SMARTS

Studying, **M**emorizing, **A**ctive Listening,
Reviewing, **T**est-Taking, and **S**urvival Skills

A Study Skills Resource Guide

By
Susan Custer
Kathy McKean
Celia Meyers
Deborah Murphy
Sylvia Olesen
Susan Parker

ISBN 1-57035-045-0

Edited by *Maureen Adams*
Text layout and cover design by *Susan Krische*
Illustrations by *Tom Oling*

Printed in the United States of America

Published and Distributed by

SOPRIS
WEST

4093 Specialty Place   Longmont, Colorado 80504   (303) 651-2829
www.sopriswest.com

10SMARTS/6-01/C&M/1M/325

Table of Contents

Introduction

The title selected for this book, *SMARTS*, refers to action steps, or skills, that will be covered in this handbook: studying, memorizing, active listening, reviewing, test-taking, and survival skills. A whole body of research indicates that these skills can be taught and that students can improve their performance in school if they learn how to study and how to remember.

The strategies and techniques advocated in *SMARTS* were originally used in resource rooms for students with mild disabilities. Field-testing in classrooms across the nation supported the theoretical research that promoted the teaching of these skills. As the authors became more involved in study skills research, it became apparent that the study skills and remembering strategies that were recommended for students with mild disabilities were also viable strategies for the general student population. *SMARTS* has been successfully used by elementary teachers as well as students in universities.

Although study skills are often taught as a separate unit of study, they are far more effective if they are taught in the content for which they will be used. Thus, each content-area teacher should determine what skills are required for success and teach those skills over the course of the year in a systematic and sequential manner, just as they teach content-related materials. As with any basic skill, students need opportunities to practice and to learn how they can improve.

Very often, students who have not experienced school success feel they have no control over the grades they make. These students credit "luck" for both their school successes and failures and see very little relationship between the things that they do and the grades that they receive. Yet, when these students are taught **what** to learn and **how** to learn, they become more willing to invest the time and effort that are necessary for greater school success. When students acquire *SMARTS*, it makes them feel more competent and makes the teacher's life far more enjoyable.

This resource guide is organized to provide awareness level activities to help both teachers and students become knowledgeable about current skill levels. It generally provides a conceptual basis for the skill acquisition as well as suggestions for additional practice appropriate for a variety of skill levels. *SMARTS* is directed toward providing students with strategies and techniques that will help them gather, record, organize, understand, remember, and use information presented in the classroom. The information presented in *SMARTS* will transfer to any content-area subject and is appropriate for diverse educational levels.

Study Skills Inventory

Self-analysis is an important step in teaching study skills. This informal inventory can reveal areas of weakness. It is designed to serve as a discussion starter to focus each student's attention on simple suggestions that can help each become a more efficient learner. They may not realize that being an efficient learner doesn't necessarily mean studying harder or longer, but rather better, in order that they remember more easily.

A discussion section on page 9 follows the Study Skills Inventory. It is written directly to the student and explains the scoring value for each inventory question item. The tone of the scoring discussion is light, but it communicates important information about study skills.

Administration of the study skills inventory without the follow-up discussion and explanation will not be an efficient use of either teacher or student time. The inventory discussion should include a group brainstorming session on what things a "good" student does to make "good" grades. Depending on the ability level and sophistication of the student group, encourage students to organize these activities into clusters or categories. This is an excellent opportunity to model or talk through categorizing skills. Use this opportunity to teach students how to think categorically.

Follow the inventory discussion and brainstorming session with the development of an official contract between you and your students to do three thing that will help the students make better grades. The contract should be for at least six weeks and should specify exactly what the student will do and what the teacher will do. Specify a reward for maintaining the contract. Many schools send a copy of the contract home to the parents; this is a positive way to involve parents in their children's school work. Many schools today are searching for ways to encourage parental participation and involvement; this activity provides an excellent vehicle for communication between the school and the home.

Study Skills Inventory

Student _____ Date _____ Class _____

Please answer the following questions. If you answer all of the questions honestly, you may be able to tell what things you can do to make studying a lot easier. CIRCLE the letter of the answer that best completes each statement.

Part I
Classroom and Study Behavior

1. When the tardy bell rings, I am usually:

   a. Outside the classroom.
   b. Inside the classroom door.
   c. In my seat.

2. When class starts:

   a. I need to borrow a pencil or paper.
   b. I need to go to my locker.
   c. I have the materials I need.

3. When class starts:

   a. My textbook is on my desk.
   b. My textbook is in my locker.
   c. I have no idea where my textbook is.

4. When it's time to turn in assignments:

   a. I pretend mine's lost because I didn't do it.
   b. I usually have mine completed.
   c. I turn in what I have even if I couldn't do it all.

5. The assignments I turn in:

   a. Are neat and legible.
   b. May be messy, but penmanship doesn't count.
   c. Are very messy. Maybe the teacher can't read it.

6. When the assignment is given to the class:

   a. I ask questions if I'm not sure I understand.
   b. I keep quiet and ask a friend later.
   c. I never ask questions; everyone else knows what to do.

7. When the teacher is talking:

   a. Sometimes I get so bored I act silly.
   b. I look like I'm paying attention.
   c. I keep up with the lecture and try to think about what is being said.

What does he mean pies are square? My mom's pies aren't square!

8. To help myself pay attention in class:

   a. I take notes about what is being said.
   b. I sit close to the front.
   c. I watch the clock to see how long I have to be still.

9. During class discussion:

   a. I keep my eyes down so the teacher won't call on me.
   b. I volunteer to answer questions or make comments.
   c. I answer if I'm called on.

10. When I have an assignment:

    a. I put it off until the last minute, but I try to finish.
    b. I plan how long it will take and schedule my time.
    c. I don't worry about it unless I get important things taken care of first.

11. My approach to studying is:

    a. To do some studying on each subject every day.
    b. I hope to pick up enough in class to pass.
    c. I try to cram it all in the night before the test.

12. When I study at home:

    a. It is in a place that I use only for studying.
    b. I try to find a quiet place.
    c. It's wherever I happen to be.

13. When I'm studying for a test:

    a. I have a good idea of what I need to learn.
    b. It seems I always study the wrong things.
    c. I make sure I know the special terms and questions in the book.

14. When I finish an assignment:

    a. I fold it carefully and put it in my book.
    b. I check over my work to make sure that it makes sense.
    c. I make sure that I didn't leave anything out.

15. The Table of Contents:

    a. Is in the back of most textbooks.
    b. Helps me to understand how topics are related.
    c. Tells what is in the book.

16. A glossary:

    a. Gives the meanings of words that the authors think are important.
    b. Can be found in every textbook.
    c. Is in the back of the book.

17. The index of a book:

    a. Is on different colored pages.
    b. Lists topics as they occur in the book.
    c. Is an alphabetical listing of topics in a book.

18. After I've read for a while:

    a. I quit so my eyes don't get tired.
    b. I ask myself questions to make sure I understand what I've read.
    c. I stop and reread when I realize I haven't understood what I read the first time.

19. While I'm reading:

    a. I take notes of things I think I'll need to remember.
    b. I think about questions that the teacher might ask.
    c. I try to finish everything at one time so I don't get mixed up.

20. Before I start reading a new chapter:

    a. I think about how long it will take so I'll make sure I have enough time.
    b. I start reading the first page and stay with it.
    c. I look through the chapter, at the pictures and the charts, and then read the summary before I get started reading the whole thing.

Part II
Taking Tests

Circle **T** for true or **F** or false for each of the following statements about taking tests.

Essay Tests

1. I read the directions and all of the questions before I start to write. **T** **F**

2. I watch the clock while I'm taking the test. **T** **F**

3. I make an outline so that I'm organized before I start writing. **T** **F**

4. If I don't know about a subject, I leave it blank so I don't sound dumb. **T** **F**

Multiple Choice Tests

5. When I decide on an answer, I never change it. **T** **F**

6. I go through and answer the ones I am sure about first. **T** **F**

7. I read all the choices before I mark an answer. **T** **F**

8. I look for clues in other questions to help answer the ones I'm not sure about. **T** **F**

9. If I don't know an answer, I eliminate the choices that don't make sense. **T** **F**

10. If I have **no** idea what the answer is on a chapter test, I mark 'C.' **T** **F**

True/False Tests

11. If I don't know the answers, I make an interesting pattern. **T** **F**

12. I look for "clue" words like **always** and **never** before I decide on the answer. **T** **F**

13. I answer the hardest questions last. **T** **F**

14. I proofread my test before I turn it in. **T** **F**

Scoring Key for Inventory

Part I	2 points	1 point	0 points
1.	c	b	a
2.	c		a or b
3.	a		b or c
4.	b	c	a
5.	a	b	c
6.	a	b	c
7.	c	b	a
8.	a	b	c
9.	b	c	a
10.	b	a	c
11.	a	c	b
12.	a	b	c
13.	a	c	b
14.	b	c	a
15.	b	c	a
16.	a	c	b
17.	c		a or b
18.	b	c	a
19.	a or b		c
20.	c	a	b

Part II	2 points	Minus 1 point
1.	T	F
2.	T	F
3.	T	F
4.	F	T
5.	F	T
6.	T	F
7.	T	F
8.	T	F
9.	T	F
10.	T	F
11.	F	T
12.	T	F
13.	T	F
14.	T	F

60-68 Points—You are a WHIZ at studying!

45-59 Points—You could probably IMPROVE your grades with a FEW study hints!

20-44 Points—You need to get SERIOUS about learning to STUDY!

10-19 Points—Aren't you glad this wasn't a REAL test?

Discussion of Items on Study Skills Inventory

Part III
Classroom and Study Behavior

1. Two points if you're in your seat. Remember that teachers are people, too. The class gets started on a more pleasant basis and you're more organized and ready to go. However, we're feeling generous, so if you're in the door, you get one point. But, you'd be better off if you changed your habits!

2.-3. Sorry, no points for anything if you don't have your materials ready for class. Without paper, pencil, textbook, or other regular materials, you'll be a loser for sure.

4. Completed assignments get two points. You learn more that way! However, if you don't finish, get credit for what you have done. One point if you turned something in—at least, you learned a little bit.

5. Neat assignments get two points. Research tells us that being neat can sometimes make a whole letter grade difference when your work is being graded. (Teachers may not even be aware of how important it is, but be honest, wouldn't you rather read something that's neat?!) But you do get one point even if it's messy. Remember, you're doing assignments to learn something.

6. Two points if you ask the teacher to clarify when you don't understand, one point if you ask a friend. The friend may not know everything either, but at least you care enough to ask!

7. Two points for keeping yourself tuned in to the lecture. You'll find you don't have to study as hard later on. You get one point for being smart enough not to be a pest. So, at least, look alert!

8. Sitting close to the front of the class is always a good idea and worth one point any day. For two points, **take notes**!

9. Two points for taking part in class discussions. It helps you learn and causes the teacher to think you are trying. If you aren't brave enough to volunteer, you get one point for answering when called on.

10. Scheduling and planning for an assignment gets you two points. You probably always get your work completed. One point for those who try to finish even if they wait until the last minute.

11. Two points for those people who know it's better to study a little every day. It's easier in the long run. One point if you at least study before the test.

12. If you always study in a special place, you get two points. It gets to be a habit to study there and you get more done. One point if you find a quiet place where you won't be interrupted.

13. Those people who have a good idea about what to study are usually the ones who take notes, keep their assignments or study guides, and study a little bit every day—they get two points. The students who have figured out that the special vocabulary terms and questions at the end of the chapter will be on the test get one point. Both groups will be in good shape at test time.

14. Two points goes to people who check their work to make sure it makes sense. It's a good study tool as well as a way to help your grade. If you at least look over your assignment to make sure you didn't leave anything out, you get one point.

15. Two points if you realize that the Table of Contents can help you understand your textbook. One point if you know it tells you what's in the book.

16. Two points if you know that the authors think the words in the glossary are important. One point if you know it may be in the back of the book.

17. The only thing you get credit for on this one is two points for knowing that an index is an alphabetical listing of topics in a book.

18. Two points if you are clever enough to ask yourself questions as you read. This is a very **powerful** tool for understanding. One point if you check yourself and reread anything you didn't understand the first time around.

19. Two points if you take notes of things you need to remember. It may sound like a lot of trouble, but it will make studying a breeze. You also get two points if you try to think of questions that the teacher might ask!

20. Two points if you remember to use SQ3R—more about that later. You get one point if you plan your time.

Essay Question Tips

1. On essay tests it's really important to read all of the questions as well as the directions. If you don't, you may find that you have put information in the wrong place.

2. Be a clock watcher. If you don't, you may spend too much time on one question and not be able to finish.

3. An outline organizes your thoughts and helps you to include all of the information.

4. Never be afraid to answer. You may get some points. If you don't answer, you don't stand a chance. Write something and try to use your best handwriting.

Multiple Choice Question Tips

1. Change your answer if you have a pretty good reason. With multiple choice questions, you may have read something while taking the test that jogged your memory.

2. You get credit for what you know. Be sure to go back through and answer something on every question.

3. Please read all the possible answers. Sometimes the wrong answers that have been put in to fool you are very tricky.

4. We hope everyone is using this little test-wise trick.

5. If you eliminate the "dumb" choices, you increase the chances that you'll choose the right answer.

6. Unless your teacher is "on to" this quirk of human nature, over 50% of the correct answers in a teacher-developed multiple choice test will be either 'B' or 'C'.

7. Don't make a pattern. Try for an "educated guess."

8. If you aren't doing this, start now.

9. You get two points for this one if you marked true. Once again, be sure you get credit for the ones you know before you start on the hard ones.

10. Yes, check your work. Make sure you didn't leave anything out. You might even find you misread a question.

True/False Tests

The Study Skills Inventory true/false questions are pretty obvious, so if your choice is wrong, you must subtract one point.

We hope you'll use the suggestions in *SMARTS* to learn to study **smarter**, not **harder**.

Previewing the Text

Learning to use textbooks is essential to becoming an independent learner. Many students reach high school without really understanding the organization of a textbook or how to use it to full advantage.

At the beginning of the year or semester, go over the book with the class. Even though previous teachers may have taught this process, you should not assume that the students have a working understanding of your book's organization. Suggestions for previewing include:

- **Go over the title page information.** As students look at the copyright date and the author, discuss point of view, time perspective, etc.

- **Look at the Table of Contents.** Have the students form opinions on how they think the material is organized. This also provides the students with a good sequential overview of the course.

- **Look at the Index together.** Explain how it can be used and offer practice in locating information by using the index.

- **Using the Index:**

  1. The index will tell you the pages on which a name or topic is mentioned in a book.

  2. If there are several references for the same topic, the references will be in alphabetical order, regardless of the page number. Here is an example:

     Leaders, military: Clark, 77; Eisenhower, 200; Gates, 65; Greene, 68; Washington, 59.

     Although Washington is mentioned in the book before the others, the listing has his name last in order. This system makes it easier to locate the particular name under the heading of military leaders.

  3. Indices have cross-references. Not all information about a topic may be listed under the heading for that topic. For example:

     Agriculture: New England, 56; South, 78. See also Farming.
     Farming: Corn, 66; Cotton, 62, 78; Tobacco, 78, 81. See also Agriculture.

- **Look at the Glossary.** Many students don't even know if their textbook has one. Some questions to include in this discussion are, "How is a glossary different from a dictionary?" and "How did the author decide which words to include?"

The students should also be introduced to the special organizational features and study aids included in their textbooks. Features such as advance organizers, chapter summaries, vocabulary lists, chapter previews, maps, charts, tables, timelines, etc. should be pointed out.

Have students bring all their textbooks to one class meeting. Discuss the study aids available in each book. Question for discussion include:

- Are words defined in the margins or must the student turn to the glossary to look up each word?

- Are all the terms for each chapter combined in one place?

- Are marginal notes used to summarize material?

- Is the chapter summary a list of main ideas or a written synopsis?

- Are special areas of information blocked off or on separate pages (lists of grammar rules, biographies, etc.)?

Have the students discuss which features are helpful and which are confusing. Have them decide which book would be easiest to study from and which would be hardest.

Group Text Inventory

After the initial introduction to the specific textbook, it would be very helpful for you to know just how well the students can use that book to find information. The following example (see Figure 1) is an inventory based on an actual history text. This format can be followed to construct an inventory based on textbooks used in your classes. The inventory would need to be constructed only once and could be used repeatedly each year the text is in use.

F I G U R E 1
Sample Group Text Inventory

This is not a test that you can fail. As an inventory, this is a measure of your ability to use your textbook and understand the information presented in it. The results may indicate ways for you to learn how to do a faster and better job with your reading assignments in social studies. Follow all directions carefully.

1. What is the name of your textbook?_____

2. Who is the author?_____

3. Which school or college does the author work for? _____

4. Who is the publisher? _____

5. What is the copyright date? _____

6. How many units are in the book? _____

7. How many chapters are in the book?_____

8. How many chapters are in Unit Three? _____

9. What era is Chapter 19 about? _____

10. Which chapter tells about WWII?_____

11. Where is the atlas? Page _____

12. Where is the biography of Karl Marx? Page _____

13. Where is a map of the Empire of Alexander the Great? Page _____

14. What is free trade?_____

    _____

    Which page did you find this information on? _____

15. Which page in the Atlas has a map of South America?_____

16. Which page would tell you about "boroughs"? _____

17. Which pages tell about craft guilds?_____

18. Which page first mentions Martin Luther? _____

19. Which pages tell about U.S. aid to Turkey? _____

20. What is the last page number in the book?_____

Listening

An Art or a Science?

Listening to learn involves using the ears and the brain. It rarely occurs naturally. Even the 15% of the population that learn best by listening need to develop better listening skills. Too many factors are busily at work to discourage effective listening. While the human brain can easily process 400 words per minute, people generally can't talk faster than about 125 words per minute. This allows the brain (this busy little organ can't tolerate boredom) to pay attention to competing stimuli and random thoughts. It is also a marvelous little association machine, and one random thought usually leads to another more interesting one, which develops into a full-blown tangent. When the brain's natural affinity for distraction is compounded by the competing interests of children and young adults, it may be a lucky accident that learning by listening takes place at all.

However, listening that leads to communication and understanding is a skill that can be taught. This implies, of course, that it can also be learned through adequate, guided practice. Since listening is a skill that is basic to the entire curriculum, every classroom provides a good laboratory for practice and development. Imagine how much easier your life could be if you faced a classroom of active listeners every day! The activities in this section were selected to help you try to create that Utopia.

Awareness Activities

The following activities are to catch each student's attention and make each aware of the importance of active listening. They point out to the students that they are not in the habit of really listening.

Activity I
Cues for Listening

This activity will help students identify the signals or cues that you send out to emphasize the important things that they will need to remember.

1. During discussion generate a list of signal cues that should alert students to take notes or pay special attention. If the discussion bogs down or the list on the chalkboard is too short, you may need to introduce additional cues. The list might include phrases such as:

   - Here are four **important** parts.
   - **Listen** to this and see if you can tell me.
   - There are three **explanations** for this.

2. After students understand the concept of listening for signal cues, assign students to keep a journal for each class for one week.

3. During that time they will record signals that their teachers have used in classes.

4. At the end of the week compare lists and discuss the cues they discovered.

As a result of this activity, your students will be more aware of what to listen for and be better prepared for additional listening exercises.

Activity II
How Do I Listen? Let Me Count the Ways

One of the best ways to make students aware of the importance of listening is to ask them how they listen. The following is a brief, nongraded inventory to get students thinking about their own listening.

How Do I Listen?

Below are statements about how you listen. Answer them true or false. There are no right or wrong answers!

1. Listening involves only your ears.   **T**   **F**

2. I listen primarily to get information.   **T**   **F**

3. I enjoy listening.   **T**   **F**

4. I listen best when I am looking at the person speaking.   **T**   **F**

5. It is hard for me to listen.   **T**   **F**

6. My emotions affect my ability to listen.   **T**   **F**

7. I take notes when I am listening.   **T**   **F**

8. I understand everything I listen to in class.   **T**   **F**

9. I ask questions when I don't understand what the teacher just said.   **T**   **F**

10. If someone is not looking at you, they are not listening.   **T**   **F**

Complete these statements:

1. I listen best when _____.

2. I would be a better listener if I_____.

3. I have to work very hard to listen to _____.

4. I enjoy listening to _____.

5. When there are a lot of distractions during a class lecture, I _____ .

6. When I need to remember what I am hearing, I _____ .

Activity III
"Dragnet"—Getting the Facts

This Activity is based on the old television series "Dragnet." Remember how Sergeant Joe Friday always asked so many questions, but had to pull out only the facts from all that information. This is an exercise in pulling out only those important facts.

Step 1:   Divide the class into small groups (four to six students).

Step 2:   Designate one student in each group to be the reader and one student to be the recorder.

Step 3:   Select a story from their reader, literature book, the newspaper, etc.

Step 4:   Have the readers read aloud to their groups.

Step 5:   Have the group discuss the details and pick out the important facts.

Step 6:   The recorder writes down the facts the group has selected. The reader may not contribute to the recording.

Step 7:   After 15 minutes (after all, there never is very much time in an investigation), the designated readers relate each group's list of important facts.

Step 8:   Discuss how the reports vary.

An interesting variation to "Dragnet" involves using the *Encyclopedia Brown* series written by Donald J. Sobol, published in paperback by the Bantam Book Company. The stories are short mysteries that are solved by the character Encyclopedia Brown using inductive thinking based on close observation of the facts. The stories stop short of giving the solution (the explanation can be found in the back of the book). When using this variation, the groups can be larger. You may wish to allow students to ask for specific parts of the story to be reread before the facts are recorded. Each group tries to solve the mystery in addition to carefully recording the facts.

Activity IV
Say What? Missing Elements

This exercise forces students to listen for details, locate the missing element(s), and make inferences.

1. Provide stories and short anecdotes in which some important element is missing. (When the fact is not included, the behavior of the characters becomes perplexing.)

2. Read the stories to the students.

3. Ask for a response.

Variations:

- Have the students make up the stories.

- Instead of reading aloud, put the stories on tape for the students to listen to individually. (Their responses could be put in a box and winners drawn out later for rewards.)

Sample Stories:

- "Wait. See there's a double space. Now, I need to shift before I try to go ahead. Yes, that margin should be wide enough. Oops, not enough room. I need to go back and adjust."

  You ask, "What machine is being used? Yes, it has keys, but it's not a car."

  (Answer: A typewriter or word processor.)

- "A girl went down to the river at the edge of town in order to listen to the river. When she came to the river bank, she heard water splashing against the rocks. Bending down to touch the ground, she knocked a pebble over the side of the bank. Seconds later, she stepped back; the color drained from her face as a gasp escaped from her ashen lips. Why?"

  (Answer: The girl was blind. Since the pebble took so long to reach the water, she realized that she was close to the edge of a high bank above the river.)

- "With a burst of speed a man ran toward home. His face showed the intensity of the effort. Seeing another man running toward him, he abruptly changed directions seeking safety from his pursuer. What is happening here?"

  (Answer: They are playing baseball.)

Activity V
Who's Paying Attention?

This technique has been shown to be effective in helping students who have difficulty controlling their attention to spend more time on task.

1. Prepare a tape that records a sound (a beep, a bell) at unequal intervals such as two minutes, five minutes, three minutes, etc.

2. Prepare a Tally Control Sheet (see sample).

3. Explain to the students that when they hear the sound, they are to ask themselves:

   - "Was I paying attention?"
   - "Was I doing what I'm supposed to be doing?"

4. Then, they are to mark their Tally Sheet: If the answer is "Yes," they place a tally mark in the "I'm Doing a Good Job" column. If the answer is "No," they place a tally in the "I Need to Get to Work "column.

5. After several sessions the record sheets can be phased out, but the students should be instructed to continue internal questions and answers when they hear the sound from the tape.

6. This can be done at any time, starting with a specific time frame, then extending throughout the day.

The self-reinforcing aspect of the personal tally control sheet (see Figure 2) is critical toward developing self-monitoring and self-control.

FIGURE 2
Personal Tally Control Sheet

I'm Doing a Good Job	I Need to Get to Work
卌	III

Activity VI
Hear Ye! Hear Ye! Questions for Listening

Try these questions on your students. These are fun, quick listening questions you can present at anytime. Before asking the questions, it is helpful to:

• Remind students that the questions will be simple and that you will read each question only once.

• Let them know that different students may get different answers because everyone listens differently. (You may want to include a discussion about how they came up with their different responses.)

• Give your students credit for different responses, especially if they can defend their reasoning.

Questions:

1. Eight buzzards sat on a telephone wire. Mr. Brown shot one of them. How many were left on the wire?

2. Correctly write fifteen thousand, five hundred, and fifteen.

3. A blizzard struck South Dakota. Steve Shepherd rescued 15 of his 50 sheep. How many sheep did Steve have left?

4. How much dirt could be found in a rectangular hole that measures four feet deep, two feet wide, and three feet long?

5. How many gummy bears can you place in an empty quart jar?

6. If you take five oranges from a box containing 30 oranges, how many do you have?

7. There are 12 penny pieces of candy in a dozen. How many nickel candies would be in a dozen?

8. How many birth dates does the average woman in the United States have?

9. Is there a Fourth of July in Australia?

10. If three women can walk two miles in 45 minutes, how far would six women, with the same ability, walk in 45 minutes?

Answer Key:

Although you probably don't need the answers to these listening questions, here they are!

1. None. The rest would fly away at the sound of the gun.

2. 15,515.

3. He saved 15.

4. There should be none in the hole.

5. None, because it would no longer be empty.

6. Five.

7. Twelve.

8. One.

9. Yes, but it isn't Independence Day.

10. Two miles.

Activity VII
Listen and Write

This exercise is for secondary school students and requires careful listening. First, have your students number their papers from 1-10. Next, caution them that each instruction will be read only once.

Instructions to be read aloud:

1. Write the first four consonants of the alphabet on line three.

2. If you are in a social studies class, write your middle name.

    If you are not, draw a diamond.

3. On line five write three forms of the word "to."

4. If Oklahoma is a country, write a 'Y' on line nine.

5. If you were facing north, write the direction that would be to your right on line ten.

6. If Shakespeare is a living author, draw a sun on line one.

7. Draw a circle that contains a rectangle. Place a triangle around the circle.

8. Complete this: In fourteen hundred and ninety-two, Columbus sailed the ocean _____.

9. If Atlantic City is the capital of New Jersey, write a 'C' on line four.

10. If the sum of 414 and 212 is greater than the sum of 412 and 214, put an 'N' on line six.

Answer Key:

1.

2. (name or diamond)

3. b,c,d,f

4.

5. to, too, two (any order)

6.

7.

8. blue

9.

10. east

If this exercise indicates that your students need more listening awareness practice, you may wish to incorporate listening exercises into your current units of study.

Here are some examples of content-area instructions to use during current units. See if you and your students can find the answers:

1. If inflation reduces the value of the dollar, put a 'V' on line three.

2. If the clavicle is a part of the respiratory system, draw an arrow pointing up.

3. If 11 is a prime number, put an 'X' on line one.

4. If your first name has an even number of letters, write the square root of 25.

5. If Brutus gave the "Friends, Romans, countrymen, lend me your ears . . . " speech, write the roman numeral five on line four.

These activities rely heavily on listening skills, but they also require reasoning and the ability to follow directions. They **should** not be used for testing content-area information, but are excellent for **review** and **practice**.

Activity VIII
Listening Rounds—Get That Message

This message chain is a primary and intermediate elementary activity that is useful for demonstrating that listening requires more than just a pair of ears. Neither encourage nor discourage the use of note-taking during the message chain. (A note-taking activity can be initiated at a later time as a technique for improving listening ability.) Steps in the message chain:

1. On a piece of paper write down a message of less than 50 words. Use events that are taking place in the school or in the classroom, but word them in such a way that close listening is required.

Examples:

- Robert's new baby brother, Jeffrey Kyle, weighed 7 lbs., 13 oz. He was born at St. Anthony's on November 12th. He is coming home tomorrow after two o'clock.

Mrs. Hopper's fourth grade class went to visit the zoo. They looked at the monkeys after they toured the tall prairie grass exhibit. They were surprised that so many different kinds and sizes of monkeys can be found in the world.

2. Read the message aloud to the first student in each row.

3. Have each of these students tell the student behind them, and so on down the row.

4. At the end of the row have the last student repeat the message to the class.

A variation might be to tell the message to several small groups, then have each group relate the message to the class.

Listening Comprehension

To be able to listen, understand, and remember, students must become more ACTIVE listeners. They need to develop compensatory listening techniques to overcome the natural internal and external distractions that are present in the classroom environment.

One such technique is the practice of **self-questioning** during lectures or teaching presentations. Researchers have verified that self-questioning is a powerful technique to help learners attend to, understand, and remember material. Also, it makes good common sense for students to learn to ask themselves questions such as the following:

1. What point is the speaker trying to make now? What do I think is being said?

2. Does this fit with what was said before? (The listener can use that extra "brain activity" to review what was said before.)

3. What do I think the speaker is going to say next? (Predicting what may come next helps the listener to stay on-task and to understand the lecture as a whole.)

4. Which words kept me from being sure I understood what was just said? (The listener should jot down the words he/she is uncertain about, and look them up later.)

Remember that you can't just tell the students that they need to ask themselves these kinds of questions. You will have to provide **guided practice** in actually using this technique in the course of your lessons. It may seem cumbersome at first when you're all fired-up to talk about the westward movement or the law of supply and demand, but you'll be pleasantly surprised that, with plenty of practice, the students will remember more with less reteaching.

At first you'll need to **model** your thought processes (i.e., talk it through for the class and encourage interactions); later, you may want to use **reciprocal** teaching, wherein you have students act as the "teacher" and supply appropriate self-questions. Finally, give credit for the recording of self-monitoring questions that students jot down during the lecture. You may want to create your own recording device, or you may choose to use some of the note-taking hints that will come later in *SMARTS* (see page 55).

Whatever system you use to teach self-questioning, be sure to give credit for vocabulary that the students record and subsequently learn in order to understand the lecture. If students can "speak the language," they can "learn the concept." Effort and time spent in developing vocabulary will pay off in better grades and greater understanding. (More about this in the section on vocabulary, page 67.)

Activity I
I Question That!

Here's a format (see Figure 3) that might be helpful for recording during self-questioning. Hand out half sheets for student responses, then once they have learned the format, keep the reminder on the chalkboard.

FIGURE 3

Self-Questioning

What Do I Think is Being Said?	What Words Kept Me From Understanding?

Activity II
Listening Posts

To help train students to think about what they are hearing, develop sentences for them to complete using cause/effect, contrasts/comparisons, and fact/opinion formats. Listening for the differences between fact and opinion will also result in a more alert listener. Teach them to listen to the signals that carry special meaning.

The sentences should be read aloud to the students, one at a time, allowing time for a response. Emphasize the "signal" words that should alert students as to the type of question—cause/effect, contrast/comparison or fact/opinion—being asked. Some discussion may follow in order to justify answers; this could be done as a class or in small groups. It can also be modified as a more creative activity in which students try to think of a response that no one else will have thought of. Don't worry if it gets a little silly.

Examples:

Cause/Effect

- **When** you drive too fast, you will probably . . .
- **When** there is an earthquake . . .
- **Since** it was raining heavily, we . . .
- **If** everyone voted, . . .
- The farmers of Oklahoma will lose 50% of their wheat crop this year **because of** . . .

Contrasts/Comparisons

- Summer is fun, **but** school is . . .
- The Fourth of July is a celebration, **and** Memorial Day is *also* . . .
- Hawaii has a tropical climate, **while** Alaska . . .
- Young people have a lot of energy; **however,** senior citizens . . .
- **Although** mass is the amount of matter in a sample, the mass number is . . .

F = Fact   O = Opinion

- The last three cars I've owned have had great sound systems in them.   ___
- Cars are equipped with great sound systems.   ___
- John has made 'A's in all his classes this year.   ___
- John is a good student.   ___
- In Geography I learned about different states and their people.   ___
- Geography is interesting.   ___
- The first paper was made by the Chinese over 2,000 years ago.   ___

- Paper has been around a long time. ___

Activity III
Read and Tell

One of the things we often forget to do at the high school level to exercise listening comprehension, is to read aloud to students. Reading interesting, motivating material to students (of all ages!) will help increase attention. The following ideas will help you to integrate reading aloud into your normal classroom routine:

- Stop throughout when reading aloud paragraphs and discuss anticipated events or outcomes.

- Have students write an appropriate headline for the article or story just read.

- Read a passage that is illogical or nonsensical, then have students talk about what doesn't make sense and why.

- Read simple directions for making or doing something (such as putting gas in a car), then have students deduce what is happening.

- Describe something, like a Sunday afternoon, or someone, like Shakespeare. Have students guess what or whom you described.

- Read a passage with an emotional content. Discuss the feelings involved.

Activity IV
Sounds All Around

Valuable sources for improving listening comprehension can be found outside the classroom. For instance, often we hear information on the radio or television without thoroughly listening to what is being said. This activity is designed to emphasize to students that active listening is something they should be practicing everywhere, not just in the classroom. The following ideas will help improve listening comprehension:

- Audiotape radio or television commercials; have students listen to them and identify what is being advertised. Have students listen for illogical or unreasonable claims.

- Give extra credit for commercials or advertisements in which students have discovered contain illogical elements.

- Play music or read lyrics from a popular song and discuss the meaning.

Activity V
Name That Character

A fun way for students to build their listening comprehension without having to listen for factual information is to use familiar nursery rhymes. Students will be listening for meaning in tone and gesture, not just words.

1. Select a favorite nursery rhyme such as, "Old Woman in a Shoe," "Little Jack Horner," or "Mary Had a Little Lamb."

2. Select students to be "character readers." (Or, you may want to record several character voices on an audiotape yourself to get your students started.)

3. Some examples of characters:

   - A preacher
   - An alien
   - The President of the United States
   - A five-year old child
   - A ghost
   - A rock music singer
   - A computer talking

4. Have the students read the nursery rhyme using a particular character's voice without identifying who they are supposed to be.

5. The listeners should then try to identify the character from gestures and tone of voice.

   (No props should be used since this is an auditory activity.)

Following Directions

If students have not learned the skill of following directions, chances are they will not be successful in their schoolwork. Following directions is an integral part of any school's curriculum; teach it as a skill. It may be overlooked in favor of other more "academic" competencies, but it is required by every teacher for assignment completion, classroom organization, and general order.

Students should be taught to read all directions before beginning a task. They need to overcome the temptation to skip the directions in order to save time. Teachers can facilitate this by giving "pop quizzes" that contain directions such as, do not complete the quiz, do only every other question, etc. If students find themselves doing extra work because they failed to read and follow the directions, they will form the habit of reading the directions first.

Activity I
Looking Back

Emphasize that it is often necessary for students to look back at the instructions while completing the work required. The following is an example to use with students:

> In the following sentences, underline the names of people once, the names of places twice, and cross out all other words in the sentence.
>
> 1. David and Jason went on a vacation to Reno, Nevada.
>
> 2. Did Sarah and Michael really go to the Springsteen concert in Dallas?
>
> 3. Next time we take a vacation to southern California, we should invite Samantha, Bob, and their children, Jacob and Michelle.

Activity II
Can You Make What I Made?

Writing out a list of directions is also a useful activity to help students pay attention to all the steps necessary for completing a task. For example, have all students write the directions for sharpening a pencil, operating a computer, or other classroom-related activities. Then exchange papers and have the students follow each other's directions exactly. The results of this kind of activity can be entertaining as well as instructional.

Activity III
Testing, Testing

Before students can follow directions, they must be able to read and understand the commonly used "direction words." Have the students look at the words and examples below; make sure they understand what they mean before starting the test.

Directions:

Study these words and examples before you begin.

circle	(word)
underline	word
box	[word]
fill in	�▌
cross out	wo̶r̶d̶
put a line over	word

Read the sentences below. Each one gives a direction. Look at the three choices that follow each question. Find the one that best shows the example and write the letter of the correct answer on the blank line.

1. Cross out the number 8.   a) ⑧   b) 8̶   c) 8   **B**

2. Put a line over the M.   a) M̶   b) M   c) M̄   **C**

3. Fill in the circle.   a) ●   b) ◗   c) ⊗   **A**

4. Put a box around the J.   a) [J]   b) J̶   c) Ⓙ   **A**

5. Circle the number 12.   a) 12   b) 1̶2̶   c) ⑫   **C**

6. Underline the biggest number.   a) ②   b) 1   c) 3   **C**

Activity IV
Directional Words

For junior or senior high students, review "test" words. Make sure that they understand what each direction word means and what it tells them to do. The following list contains suggested terms:

Clue Word	What To Do
Analyze	Tell about the main ideas, how they are related, and why they are important.
Comment on	Discuss, criticize, or explain the subject.
Compare	Show how things are similar.
Contrast	Show how things are different.
Criticize	Evaluate something on the basis of its strengths and weaknesses.
Define	Give the meaning of something.
Describe	Write detailed information about something.
Diagram	Make a graph, chart, or drawing; label it and write a short explanation.
Discuss	Give details of an idea and explain the good and bad of each.
Enumerate	Name or list the main ideas one by one.
Evaluate	Give your own judgment or relate an expert's opinion of how important an idea is; explain strengths and weaknesses.
Illustrate	Explain by giving examples.
Interpret	Give the meaning by using examples or personal ideas.
Justify	Give reasons why you think an idea is important.
List	Write down and number.
Outline	Write main ideas in organized order.
Prove	Show by logic or reason that something is true (this word has a special meaning in math and physics).
Relate	Describe how things are connected or how one thing can cause another.
Review	Give a summary by telling the important parts.
State	Describe as clearly as you can.
Summarize	Give a short list or explanation of the main ideas.
Trace	Follow the progress or history of an idea.

For students who have difficulty memorizing a lot of words and definitions, have them concentrate on the seven most frequently used direction words:

- Discuss
- Contrast
- Compare
- Describe

- Criticize
- List
- Define

A good extension activity for your more advanced students would be to have them write the meanings of these additional terms:

- Pros and cons
- Sequence
- Concept
- Concrete examples
- Summary

- Omit
- Similarities
- Survey
- Differences
- Be precise

Activity V
Idiomatic Directions

The English language is full of phrases whose directions can't be followed. Idioms add color and flare to our language, but they can be confusing when trying to follow directions. You may want your students to try to translate these "Idiomatic Directions" by rewriting the following lecture. For extra credit, let students write their own scenarios using idioms. Younger children may enjoy illustrating idioms literally. The idioms used in the sample lecture below are underlined.

> <u>Give me a break!</u> Your grades could be better so <u>listen up</u> and <u>get your act together</u>. If you don't <u>watch your step</u>, you'll find that your grades are <u>the pits</u>. Let's <u>talk turkey</u> and come to a <u>meeting of the minds</u>. I could stand here and <u>read you the riot act</u>, but I'm afraid you'd just <u>throw in the towel</u>. It's <u>not the end of the world</u>, so don't <u>fly off the handle</u>. If you just <u>knuckle under</u> and learn to study a little, you'll be on <u>top of the world</u>.

Activity VI
Directions Without Hearing

Assigning a project that students can take home with them is always a popular activity. Writing the step-by-step instructions on the board or a flip-chart will help students learn the importance of following directions. For younger students, draw a picture of the assigned project next to the instructions. For example:

My Pet Rock

You will need:

1. A mixing bowl
2. ¼ cup liquid white glue
3. ¼ cup powdered tempera paint
4. Piece of wax paper
5. Paint brush (½" to ¾" wide)
6. Medium to large size rock
7. Picture of yourself

Directions:

1. Mix paint and glue together in the bowl.
2. Put the rock on the wax paper.
3. Paint the rock with the paint-glue mixture.
4. Put the picture on the wet rock.
5. Let your pet rock dry.

Older students can enjoy this activity, too. Discuss what different colors are made by mixing two different colors together, or what the white color of the glue does to the intensity of the color, or other interesting transformations that have taken place.

Activity VII
Content Stuff

Following directions is a natural skill that can be taught in science (experiments), home economics (recipes), social studies (maps, charts), and math (formulas, equations). Use your imagination! Develop some discussion. Here are some thought provoking questions that will engage students in using their listening, reasoning, and discussion skills:

- What do you think would have happened if early explorers hadn't followed the directions on their maps and charts?

- If you didn't follow the directions for making a chocolate cake, would it be a chocolate cake?

- What would happen if scientists didn't follow the exact formula for making jet fuel?

Activity VIII
Hide and Seek

Involve your students in a scavenger hunt. For elementary students, reinforce directions with clues such as, "Look under the chair," "Go to the red box on the shelf," etc. (That's also a great way to introduce prepositions!) Older students would enjoy clues written in verse, code, or a foreign language (when appropriate). Make sure the last item in the hunt is worth something to the students.

Activity IX
Where Am I?

After a geography lesson, photocopy a portion of the map, preferably one without obvious clues like major cities. Tell the students they are lost and have them write down specific instructions describing what they would do to find their way home.

Activity X
"Puzzle Me Out"

The directions for this kind of activity must be followed exactly or the final product will not produce a picture. There are numerous commercial books available which include this kind of game; we have included a sample to illustrate the point.

Directions:

Read each of the following sentences. To the left of each sentence is a part of speech. Count how many times that part of speech appears in the sentence. Write that number on the line following the sentence. Each number corresponds to a color. If you have correctly counted each part of speech and then color the corresponding number, a picture will appear in Figure 4.

Example:

Pronouns	He gave Mary the book. 1	(1 = yellow)

1 = Yellow   2 = Black   3 = Orange   4 = Blue   5 = Green
6 = Brown   7 = Pink

Nouns	I bought a new couch, table, and four chairs for the living room in my house. _____
Adverbs	Jacob ran quickly up the steps, dashed through the door, and ate his dinner very fast. _____
Conjunctions	The plane and the train were both late. _____
Adjectives	The beautiful lights on the Christmas tree twinkled like fireflies on a cold, snowy night. _____
Verbs	The old car coughed and sputtered. _____

FIGURE 4

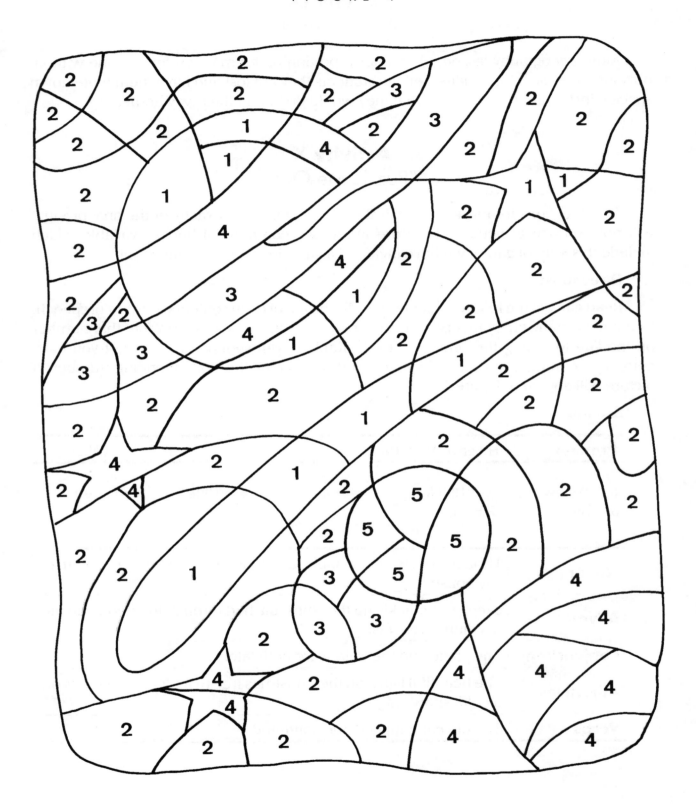

Activity XI
Geoboard Fun

Here's a following directions activity using geoboards.

1. Have students create designs with colored rubber bands on geoboards.

2. Pass out geo-grid papers (you can make your own) so that students can use colored pencils to duplicate their own designs. Check each for accuracy.

3. Using coordinates and colors, students write out directions for duplicating their design.

4. Have students switch instructions and try to replicate each other's designs. It may be more interesting to have students from another class try this. It is a great activity for open house or parents' night. Let the parents try to follow the directions and create the design.

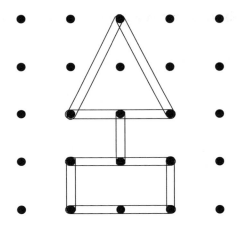

Activity XII
Directions for Paragraphs

This activity is designed to enhance your students' abilities to follow directions as well as paragraph development skills. First, provide students with a topic (e.g., New Year's Eve), then take them verbally through the following eight steps.

1. "In your **first** sentence introduce three ideas."

    (e.g., On New Year's Eve our family went to the celebration downtown, ate foods from around the world, and saw several performances.)

2. "In your **second** sentence, tell something about the first idea."

    (e.g., My sister and her daughter went with us.)

3. "In your **third** sentence, tell something else about the first idea."

   (e.g., It was my niece's birthday.)

4. "In your **fourth** sentence, tell something about the second idea."

   (e.g., We tasted food from Germany and India.)

5. "In your **fifth** sentence tell something else about the second idea."

   (e.g., We even had some fried ice cream!)

6. "In your **sixth** sentence tell something about the third idea."

   (e.g., There was a musical group playing songs from the 1950s.)

7. "In your **seventh** sentence tell something else about the third idea."

   (e.g., We saw a one-act play in which all the actors were children.)

8. Your **eighth** sentence should be a summary of the other seven sentences.

   (e.g., "We were all tired when we got home; it was quite a celebration!")

Organizational Skills

Many students have difficulties with tasks involving organization of time and materials. Teaching tactics such as utilizing organizational notebooks, assignment sheets, and basic study skills can greatly improve your students' abilities to organize, and therefore achieve.

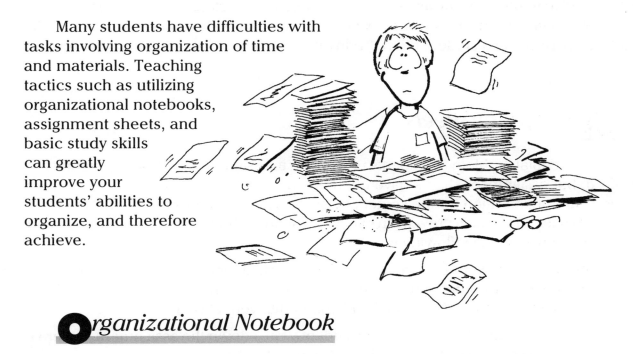

Organizational Notebook

Success for students having difficulties with organization may be facilitated by teaching such skills as notebook organization. With organizational notebooks, teachers and students have a system to assure that all activities and homework assignments have been copied accurately and thus, returned at the proper time.

The organizational notebook minimizes the problems associated with students afflicted with "Disorganizational Syndrome." Almost everything students need, with the exception of textbooks, is contained in one package. The materials needed to create an organizational notebook are as follows:

1. One three-ring binder to hold all materials.

2. One paper calendar with the current month attached on the inside cover of the notebook for assignment due dates.

3. One plastic pouch for pencils, erasers, pens, cards, etc.

4. Two pencils or pens.

5. One portfolio (folder with pockets) for each class to hold assignments, study guides, etc.

6. Loose-leaf paper or a spiral notebook for each class.

7. One copy of the How To Use SQ3R With Textbooks handout (see page 50) taped to inside back cover for easy reference.

The organizational notebook has proven effective for both elementary and secondary students. A homework assignment sheet is maintained for each class. At first, points may be awarded to reinforce using and bringing the notebook to class. (Example: Bringing the notebook to class everyday is worth six points on an end of the unit exam.) Never take points away because a student did not bring the notebook. It should only have positive connotations.

Assignment Sheets

The perennial problem of students not turning in assignments cannot be completely resolved, but assignment sheets have been the answer for many students. The sheets provide easy organization for the student because all assignments for the day are listed on a single sheet. They also provide an excellent means of home-school communication. The system works in the following way:

1. At the beginning of each school day, the student picks up his/her blank assignment sheet from the counseling office or homeroom teacher. (See page 43 for an assignment sheet that can be distributed to your class.)

2. Before the end of each class, the student writes down the assignment. If there is no assignment, the student writes, "No Assignment."

3. The teacher carefully checks to make sure the correct assignment has been recorded. Once the teacher has initialed the box, whatever is written in the "assignment" area is the homework assignment for that day. If the student brings in the wrong assignment, his/her work is compared with what is written on the assignment sheet.

4. When the student gets home, a parent initials the assignment sheet. The parent is then aware of the student's assignments for **each** day.

5. It is then the student's responsibility to complete the assignments, bring them to school, and turn in the previous day's completed assignment sheet before picking up a new one.

The parents and school work together to ensure that more assignments are completed. Each party's responsibility is clear and time is not wasted on deciding whether or not the student had assignments, who did or did not have knowledge of the assignment, etc. In addition, some students use the assignment sheets to set up goals for studying. They can review all assignments at once, rank their importance, estimate how long it will take to finish, and begin studying.

Date _____

Daily Assignment Sheet

	Teacher Initial	Parent Initial
First-hour subject _____ Assignment _____ _____ Date due _____		
Second-hour subject _____ Assignment _____ _____ Date due _____		
Third-hour subject _____ Assignment _____ _____ Date due _____		
Fourth-hour subject _____ Assignment _____ _____ Date due _____		
Fifth-hour subject _____ Assignment _____ _____ Date due _____		
Sixth-hour subject _____ Assignment _____ _____ Date due _____		

Instant Study Skills

Many students do not know how to study. They are expected to learn to study without being taught how to do it. The first week of the semester is the perfect time to teach students study skills because the basics require little time investment from the student. The following handout (pages 45-47) is written directly to the student and may be distributed to your class.

Let your students know that there are things they can do to make studying easier. Better study habits can mean better grades! They have nothing to lose and might gain a lot. Go ahead—Try it!

Instant Study Skills

Here you have a set of instant study improvement techniques. Each of them is designed to improve your grades and make studying a little bit easier without any extra time devoted on your part. These techniques certainly can't hurt you. And as long as you have to put the time in anyway, why not?

In the Classroom

Sit as close to the teacher as you can on the first day of class.

Do you know that students who sit closer to the teacher get better grades? Perhaps that's true because often the people who choose to sit closer to the front are the more serious students (they would get good grades no matter where they sat in the classroom). However, there is some evidence that regardless of ability, students can increase their chances for a good grade by sitting closer to the teacher. The closer you sit, the fewer visual distractions there are. The fewer the distractions, the easier it is to concentrate and take notes. And to cap it off, you are much less likely to daydream, read a paper, or write letters if you are under the instructor's eye. So, sit as close as you dare. If the seating is assigned, wear glasses and plead near-sightedness. Just get up front!

Why would you sit there on the first day? Because students are creatures of habit; you tend to use the same seat automatically. Did you ever notice that you step over the same feet and bump into the same knees going to your seat every day? Seating position tends to be a habit. Use it to your best advantage. Sit up front and establish the habit early!

Review previous class notes occasionally.

Let's be honest. Everyone gets bored occasionally in class, even the teacher. If you're bored in a lecture, don't doodle in your notebook or write letters. Flip through your previous class notes. You are in the classroom anyway, so you may as well be productive. Looking over previous notes may generate some interest and help get you back on the track with the lecture. Even if the teacher continues to "ramble" and you continue to be disinterested, reviewing previous notes will be a good way to get ready for upcoming examinations. The more you review, the more material you will retain for later use on exams.

Copy down everything from the board.

Did you ever stop to think that every blackboard scribble may be a clue to an exam item? If you copy it, it may serve as a useful clue for you later in reviewing. If what the teacher says doesn't seem to agree with what he/she has written on the board, or if you can't see how it relates, jot down a word or two from the board in the margin of your notes. A single word may be useful to you later. If not, you haven't wasted anything. You were in the classroom anyway.

Study and Concentration

Find a place for study and nothing but study.

Do you have a place for study you can call your own? As long as you are going to study, you may as well use the best possible environment. Of course, it should be reasonably quiet and relatively free from distractions like radio, TV, and people. (But that is not absolutely necessary. Several surveys suggest that 80% of a student's study is done in his/her own room, not in a library or study hall.)

A place where you are used to studying and not doing anything else is the best of all possible worlds for a student. After a while you'll get so used to studying there, the behavior will become almost automatic. Then whenever you sit down in your study spot, you'll feel like going right to work. Look at it this way, when you come into a classroom you sit down and go to work by paying attention to the teacher. Your attitude, attention, and behavior are automatic because in the past the classroom has been associated with attentive listening. If you can arrange the same kind of situation for the place where you study, you will find it easier to sit down and start studying.

Before you begin an assignment, write down the time when you expect to be finished (your goal time).

This one step will not take any time at all. However, you will find it can be extremely effective. It may put just the slightest bit of pressure on you, enough so that studying will become more efficient. Keep the sheets of paper where you have recorded your goal time as a record of your study efficiency. Try setting slightly higher goals on successive evenings. Don't try to make fantastic increases in rate, just push the goal up a bit at a time.

If you are not paying attention to your assignment, stand up and face away from your books.

Don't just sit at your desk staring into a book and mumbling about your poor will power. If you do, your textbook soon becomes associated with daydreaming and guilt. If you must daydream, and we all do it occasionally, get up and turn around.

Don't leave the room. Just stand by your desk, daydreaming while you face away from your assignment. The physical act of standing up helps bring your thinking back to the job. Try it! You'll find that soon just telling yourself, "I should stand up now" will be enough to get you back on track with your assignment.

Stop at the end of each page and count to ten slowly when reading.

This is an idea that may increase your study time, but it will be quite useful to you if you find you can't concentrate and your mind is wandering. If someone were to ask you, "What have you read about?" and the only answer you could give is "About 30 minutes," then you need to apply this technique. But remember, it is only useful if you can't concentrate, as a sort of emergency procedure.

Review your reading or assignment quickly before you go on to something else.

Few students realize that a short, immediate review is their very best study time investment. However, you will find that the few minutes you take flipping through an assignment before you start something new will aid you tremendously in retaining the material for future review. Research indicates that a brief review at the end of a study assignment is much more efficient than the same amount of time spent in review later on. The immediate review is terribly important.

Underlining

Never underline a whole sentence.

Many students underline as they are reading. They underline whole sentences and in some cases whole paragraphs. For the most part, they are wasting their time. If you underline (research indicates this is the most efficient way to take notes), underline only after you have read the material. Go back and pick out a few words that summarize the author's main point. Never underline a whole sentence. If you do, you will not be forced to select from the material that seems most important to you.

None of these study skills will take a lot of time and if you apply them to your existing homework routine, you will be pleased with the payoff!

Using Textbooks Effectively

The textbook is the central focus of students' learning experiences. Too often, students passively read the assigned pages or answer the assigned questions without really thinking about what is being read. Particularly in books with long chapters, students may lose the overall concepts by concentrating on memorizing facts in each chapter.

The activities in this section are designed to help students learn to become active readers by:

- **Thinking** about the information as they read.
- **Relating** new material to previously learned material.
- **Forming** questions to further their learning.

SQ3R—Survey, Question, Read, Recite, Review

SQ3R is based the information-processing theory of learning. Each component of SQ3R serves to facilitate the processing of information, which in turn should improve recall of the material being presented. The procedure was developed by F.P. Robinson in 1946, but many variations of it have appeared over the years. The original method is presented here, but if you prefer a variation such as PQRST, that method can be substituted. The main principle is that students take a more active role in reading their textbooks.

The first two steps (Survey and Question) should be taught and utilized first. These two steps are the most crucial in getting the student to actively read. The Recite and Review components encourage evaluation and selection of the most relevant information, slow down the input of information to allow time to transfer information from short-term to long-term memory, and interfere with the forgetting process. Each step must be modeled by the teacher; merely describing the steps is not enough. It is best to have students form small groups and work on one or two of the steps at a time. (Students seem to find the Question phase difficult, so extra emphasis should be placed on this component.) After the initial lessons on SQ3R, structure assignments in such a way as to encourage students to apply the method on their own.

The following is a student handout that may be duplicated for use in learning and applying SQ3R.

How To Use SQ3R With Textbooks

Survey:
- Find the pages of your assignment.
- Estimate how long it will take to do the work.
- Think about how much time you will spend on it now.
- Study the title.
- Change the title to a question.
- Think about what the words mean.
- Skim through the assignment.
- Look at subheadings, charts, maps, and pictures.
- Read the chapter summary or the last paragraph.
- Read the questions at the end of the chapter.

Question:
- Turn the headings or subheadings into questions.
  (e.g., "Food Crops of Africa" becomes "What are the food crops of Africa?")
- Write down some of the questions so you can remember them later.

Read:
- When you read, ask: "What is the writer trying to tell me?"; "What am I supposed to do?"; or "Is this fact or opinion?"
- If you don't know what a word means by the way it is used, write the word.
- Later, look in a dictionary for the meaning.

Recite:
- Show yourself and your teacher what you have learned:
  - You can answer questions in class.
  - You can write a report about what you have read.
  - You can outline what you have read.
  - You can take a test over what you have read.

Review:
- It is important to review after you have finished reading the assignment.
- Close your book and see how much you can remember.
- Go back to the important things you may have forgotten.
- Think about how the information you read has given you the main ideas.
- You may want to take notes after reading and reviewing each part of the assignment.

Answering Chapter Questions

The questions at the end of each chapter should be more than just "busy work" for the students. Used properly, they can increase reading comprehension by providing a purpose for reading. Research has shown that students comprehend more if they are reading in order to answer a question instead of passively going through the material. It helps them focus their concentration as well as break the chapter into smaller, more easily understandable pieces. The format shown in Figure 5 can serve as a guideline for reading the chapter and answering questions. This information can be read aloud, written on the board, or given to the students as a handout.

FIGURE 5

Remember: The questions in the back of the chapter usually follow the order in which the information is presented in the chapter.

1.   Turn to the back of the chapter and read the first question.

2.   Then, turn to the beginning of the chapter and start reading until you find the answer to the first question.

3.   Write it down.

4.   Find the answer to each question using steps 1, 2, and 3.

Hint: Keep a bookmark in the textbook where the questions are, and another marker where you are reading, so you can quickly refer back and forth.

Color-Coding Textbooks

Frequently, up to 50% of the students in an upper-grade class cannot read their textbooks. This is not to suggest that these students cannot read, it just means that literacy does not guarantee success with all types of reading assignments. Ability to simply read material does not ensure that students are proficient enough to learn effectively from a content-area textbook. Utilizing color-coding may help improve comprehension and recall. This simple technique emphasizes the important information to be learned, as well as providing you with a method of reviewing the information, organizing lectures, and preparing examinations.

Ideally, the content-area teacher will color-code the textbook. This can be done when you are reviewing the chapter prior to teaching the unit. If another person such as an aide is doing the color-coding, the material to be highlighted may come from the questions at the end of the chapter or from a study guide provided by the teacher. Don't overhighlight the text. Color-coding too much of the material is counterproductive.

The volume of material to be studied is reduced and studying becomes a worthwhile task once the student knows exactly what to study. A slow or low-level reader also benefits by being able to gain information from the highlighted material. Color-coded texts also provide an excellent guide for test review. Students using color-coded texts have found that studying in this fashion does pay off. As a result, their overall study habits and attitudes improve.

For example, three different colors of highlighting pens can be used in the following manner:

- Green for vocabulary words and terms.
- Pink for definitions.
- Yellow for facts, names, dates, and topic sentences.

Provide a key in the front of textbooks for students as a reference to the color scheme and always use the same colors so that students will not become confused from one text to the next. Students can also highlight their own texts with directions from you. At the end of the school year, you will have a classroom set of highlighted textbooks that will benefit students for several years and your students will have developed a valuable study technique.

Using Graphs and Charts

Most textbooks, especially in the areas of science and social studies, use graphs and charts to summarize or convey information. Students routinely seem to ignore this information in their texts unless there is a specific reason for using it (such as a chapter question). The difficulty in teaching students about graphs and charts is that the material is nearly always taught in isolation, unrelated to material that students experience daily. The students are missing a valuable study aid as well as a skill that might help them in writing reports or making oral presentations.

Students should be taught not only how to read graphs or charts, but also how to interpret them. This is much like teaching them to "read between the lines" in a literature assignment. The study of graphs should include pictographs, bar graphs, line graphs, and circle graphs. Practice in interpreting graphs begins simply and moves to complex interpretations. The following might be a sequence for a unit on line graphs:

1. Explanation of a simple single-line graph of a student's grade average.

2. Study of a graph with a single line that steadily increases.

3. Practice with lines that show increases, decreases, and leveling off.

4. Fraction of a graph with two lines comparing and contrasting information.

Timelines

A timeline is a specialized graph that is often used in textbooks to place events in chronological order. Many students ignore timelines in social studies texts simply because they do not understand them. The timeline should be taught initially through the use of boxes that represent a single year. This concept is more easily understood when students make a timeline of important events in their own lives (see Figure 6). For example:

FIGURE 6

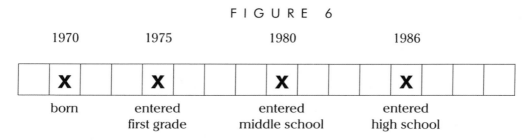

After students understand the basic concept, have them construct timelines based on other events. As they learn to understand the concept of a timeline, the boxes for each year are discarded and events are displayed both above and below the timeline (see Figure 7). Finally, they are asked to interpret historical events by using the timelines in their textbooks. In their study of timelines, students should be required not only to recognize specific periods, years, and events on a timeline, but also to understand relationships between events. Once students understand timelines, they will be able to use them (or construct them) as study aids.

F I G U R E   7

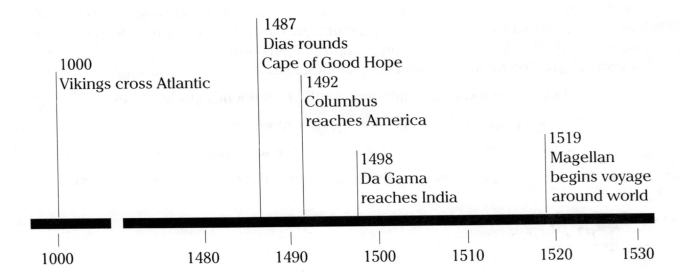

Note-Taking

Students should be actively involved when listening to lectures, watching films, and reviewing or reading materials. Listing, underlining, and outlining are just a few of the methods students can use to become actively involved in the material they are trying to learn and remember. In addition, students need to be encouraged to take notes whenever they will need to **recall** or **review** material. The note-taking system utilized should be simple, consistent, complete, and personal. This section provides several suggestions on how to instruct students to take effective notes.

Four Important Factors in Note-Taking

1. **Preparation**

   Preparation is essential for efficient notetaking. If the students are prepared, they will be able to anticipate what is going to be covered in class. This can prevent confused or erratic note-taking. If the students are familiar with the material, they can spend more time listening and less time writing down unimportant details. If there is no reading assignment, reviewing the previous day's notes should be helpful in setting the frame of reference for the lecture. Also, being on time and having all the necessary materials are an additional two factors essential in preparation.

2. **Concentration**

   The typical person thinks four times faster than a speaker can talk. This fact makes it easy for students' minds to wander during a lecture. To improve concentration, instruct your students to:

   - Try to anticipate what the speaker is going to say.
   - Try to organize the ongoing lecture with an outline.
   - Listen or watch for clues that identify the speaker's main points.

3. **Selection**

   It is physically impossible for students to write down everything a teacher says. Even if it were possible, it wouldn't be a good idea. The key to good note-taking is selection. Encourage students to continually ask themselves, "Does this really relate to the subject at hand?" For your part, when speaking emphasize clue words to indicate that your are making an important point. Specific phrases such as "We're going to cover . . . " or "The first aspect of . . . " are clues that will help students organize their notes. You can also slow down your rate of speech when presenting an important point. In addition, encourage students to copy down everything on the chalkboard.

4. **Usable Form**

Students should be taught several forms that can be used to take notes so that they can pick or adapt a form that is easy for them to use. Students who write illegibly when rushed will probably have to rewrite their notes so they can be read later. Rewriting or summarizing should be done as soon as possible after class. You should initially provide time for this at the end of class so that students will begin to build a habit of reworking their notes.

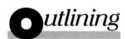utlining

Outlining is an excellent way to identify main ideas and important supporting details. However, many students have never learned how to outline. One reason is that outlining is usually taught in conjunction with isolated reading or English activities. The students need to be directed and taught how to outline content-area materials. Outlining then becomes relevant and the students will be able to apply it for taking notes.

A good way to begin teaching outlining is to prepare an outline of the material to be covered. If the lesson is to be in a lecture format, you can construct the outline on the chalkboard or on an overhead transparency. In this case, all students should copy the information. For those students who have severe handwriting, processing, or copying problems, a clear copy of the outline can be provided by you or another student by using carbonless paper. This paper can make up to five copies at one writing. Carbonless paper is quite inexpensive and only requires a special notebook to hold the paper and protect the paper supply while it is being used. It can be found at most office supply stores and bookstores. It is also available from:

Campus Connections Bookstore
Rochester Institute of Technology
48 Lomb Memorial Drive
Rochester, NY 14623-5604
Phone: (716) 475-2504

Many schools provide photocopies of either teachers' notes or other students' notes to those who can't study from their own notes. However, it is very important for those students with difficulties to try to take notes and trade these efforts for the clearer copy.

Outline Format

When presented with the task of outlining, many students may vaguely remember some sort of structure or framework they are supposed to follow, yet are not sure enough to attempt it. The standard outline format shown in Figure 8 should be presented to the students as a "map" to follow when taking notes. Have students tape a copy of an outline map in their notebooks for easy referencing.

FIGURE 8

I. MAIN IDEA

    A. Detail

    B. Detail

        1. sub-detail

        2. sub-detail

Allow students to practice using the standard outline format by providing a paragraph from their textbooks, having them complete the outline, and then checking it as a group. This will give the students who are unsure of their understanding of this standard format a chance to know, finally, what it is they are supposed to do. Keep in mind that outlining only works with material that is very organized. For material that is spontaneous, random, or disorganized, other forms of note-taking should be used.

Slot Outline

The slot outline is another way to ease students into outlining. The students simply fill in the blanks of skeleton outlines (provided by you) during the lecture or reading lesson (see Figure 9). When the outlines have been checked for accuracy, the students have a good study guide and are learning how to outline as well.

FIGURE 9

Sample Slot Outline

<u>MUSCLES</u>

I. Definition: Muscles are _____which move body parts.

II. Numbers: About _____ muscles in human body
    About _____% of male weight
    About _____% of female weight

III. Types: Voluntary_____be controlled
                   Example:_____
                   _____cannot be controlled
                   Example:_____

<u>THREE KINDS OF MUSCLES</u>

I. Smooth Muscles

    A. Involuntary
    B. Line walls of internal_____
    C. Example:_____

II. Striated Muscles

    A. _____
    B. Have bands called_____
    C. Also called_____
    D. Attached to bones by _____
    E. Move bones and limbs by _____and relaxing

III. Heart (_____) muscles

    A. Involuntary
    B. Has_____
    C. Only in _____
    D. Contracts and relaxes to _____

Content Mapping

Content mapping is a way to take notes from material that is less organized. These maps can take on several forms depending on the individual and/or the content of information presented. Three forms of content mapping are presented in Figures 10-12. Steps to present to students are as follows:

1. In capital letters, print the central idea of the lecture, text, or discussion.

2. Put important ideas or facts on a line that's connected to the main idea.

3. Put supporting details on lines connected to ideas they describe.

FIGURE 10

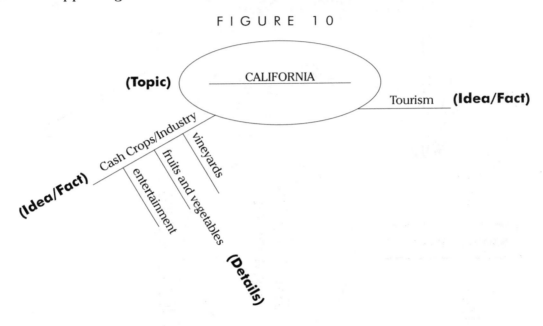

Remember: All notes should be connected in a way that makes sense to the user.

FIGURE 11

An Example of a Completed Content Map of a Discussion on
Food Chains or Food Webs

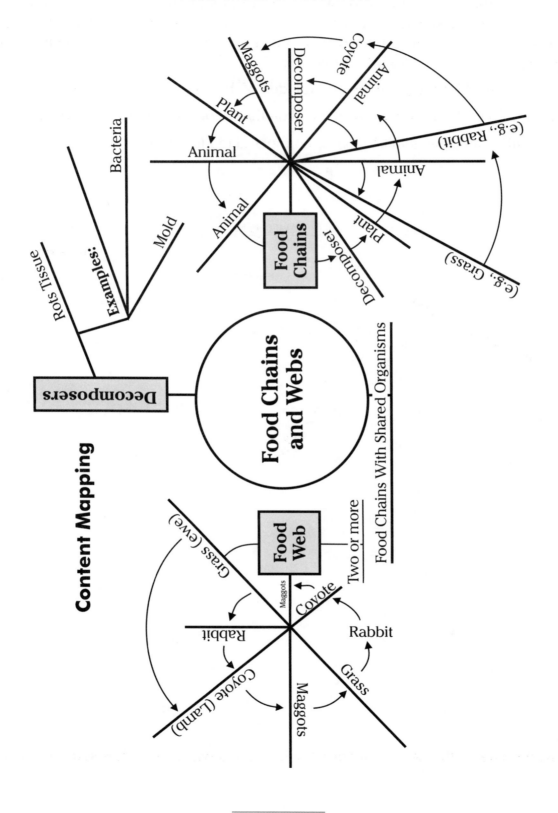

Herringbone Technique

The herringbone technique is another form of outlining that helps students organize information. Its name comes from the configuration of the outline in the shape of a fish skeleton (see Figure 12).

When instrumenting students on creating a herringbone outline, have them answer these questions as they read:

1. **What** is the main idea?
2. **Who** was involved?
3. **What** did they do?
4. **When** was it done?
5. **Where** was it done?
6. **How** did they do it?
7. **Why** did it happen?

FIGURE 12

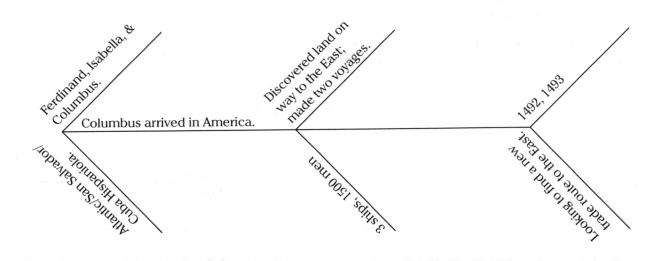

Note Frame

If students are going to take useful notes, and if the standard outline format is not desired, they need to be provided with an alternative note-taking framework, along with guided practice. The note frame technique (see Figure 13) is one such alternative that the authors have found helpful for material presented in either a verbal or written form. The steps are as follows:

- The page number is jotted down so the student can easily find the material in the text if the notes are unclear or more explanation is needed.

- A column is provided for special vocabulary that the student needs to learn.

- The notes in the middle column can be written in any format. If the student has learned the standard format, it should be used.

- The right hand column can be used for review. The student rewrites the notes into possible test questions. When it's time to study for a test, the student folds down the line between the sample question and the notes to form an effective study guide. This method provides self-checking and immediate reinforcement while studying the important information.

Time should be provided for students to go over notes in class to ensure that the main points and pertinent information are included.

FIGURE 13

Sample Note Frame

		Class _____
		Period _____
		Date _____

Topic _____

Page	Vocabulary	Notes	Sample Questions

Paragraph Study Sheet

The paragraph study sheet (see Figure 14) can help students when they need to take notes from written material for a theme or written report. It provides the students with a very structured way to study and paraphrase information. Those students who would be lost if they were asked to summarize or paraphrase information, can complete the paragraph study sheet. By answering all the questions provided, they have selected the important information from the material and can use the completed study sheet for further study, or as the basis for a written assignment.

FIGURE 14

Sample Paragraph Study Sheet

Topic Sentence: _____

_____

_____

Details:

Who? _____

_____

_____

What? _____

_____

_____

Where? _____

_____

_____

When? _____

_____

_____

Why? _____

_____

_____

How? _____

_____

_____

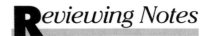eviewing Notes

An Annotation System

After students have taken notes in class or during assignment reading, they should use some sort of marking system to make the notes more useful. Annotated notes make reviewing easier while the process of selecting the material for special marking provides a good short-term review. Ideas for marking notes to present to your students include:

    ⬭   circle main idea

[   ]   bracket major supporting details

‾‾‾‾‾‾‾‾   underline minor supporting details

▭   box important names, dates, and places.

For Example:

> **Notes:**
> In [New Orleans] on [December 20, 1803]—(American flag raised over Louisiana Territory.)
>
> Jefferson chose [Meriwether Lewis] and [George Rogers Clark] to explore the new area. Started in [St. Louis] in [1804] going by boat up Missouri River. Were supposed to note different Indians and make friends with them.
>
>   [Sacajawea]—a Shoshone who had been captured as a child became interpreter.
>
>   On [November 7] they reached the [Pacific Ocean].
>
>   Built Fort Clatsip—named after local Indians.
>
>   On [September 23,] 1806 they returned to mouth of Missouri River at [St. Louis.]

Teachers often find that a system developed in the classroom is more effective as a study tool. Be sure to include credit for the annotated notes if you want your students to study from them.

In Summary

Students who take notes of any kind—even if it's a simple list, notes in the margin of the book, or in a personalized random style—are aided tremendously in the recall process. The actual note-taking interferes with the forgetting process. When students go over the notes, organize them, and make sense of them, it contributes to a higher level of comprehension and recall.

As the teacher, you need to emphasize the value of note-taking by discussing what is expected and showing students how to take notes. Symbols and abbreviations that are common to that particular content should be taught. You should also use physical and verbal cues to signal important information during lecture periods. Here are a few concrete suggestions for making sure that students take notes:

- Weekly review of notes.
- Review notes with a partner in class.
- Use notes during games.
- Give extra credit for notes.
- Give occasional unannounced open-note quizzes.
- Use notes for group preparation of different types of test questions.

Building Vocabulary

Key words or terms in texts are often emphasized by underlining, putting them in italics, boldface print, or setting them off by dashes. Students need to be tuned in to these "pay attention" signs. If they do something with these special words, such as putting them on index cards or listing them in a content-area notebook, they'll be making the first step toward integrating the word into their vocabulary.

Different subjects require specialized vocabulary. For example, to understand social studies you need to understand special words. Here are seven ways to build vocabularies, using social studies as an example:

1. Classify words into topic areas.

   Example:

Government	Economics	Geography
judicial bureaucrat	recession inflation	topography latitude

2. Use context clues to figure out special meanings.

   Example:

   Compact (as in "the Mayflower *compact* marked an important step in creating the first government") means something very different from compact in cosmetology or science.

3. List names, places, or events that relate to a word.

   Example: compact—relates to Pilgrims.

4. Link a word with other words that relate to the same time in history.

   Example: fascism, World War II, stormtroopers, nationalism.

5. Think of other forms of a word.

   Example: economy, economize, economical.

6. Use the keyword mnemonic method described in the memory section (see page 75).

7. Use crossword puzzle study guides to encourage learning the important vocabulary (see Figure 15).

FIGURE 15

American History—The Spirit Grows
Chapter 12

ACROSS CLUES

1. These tales by James Fenimore Cooper are about American frontiersmen.

5. Person who believes all people are socially, politically, and economically equal.

7. This declaration is about equality for women.

8. Machine that cuts grain or harvests a crop.

DOWN CLUES

2. Boat powered by steam.

3. This group lived in Massachusetts and was made up of American writers.

4. Undertaking big new projects.

6. Improving conditions by changing them.

Answers:

(1) Leatherstocking   (4) enterprise   (7) Sentiments
(2) steamboat   (5) egalitarian   (8) reaper
(3) Concord   (6) reform

Classifying

Classifying is a great way to build concepts. Everyone is right, students work together, and critical thinking occurs. An example classifying exercise appears below.

Procedure:

1. **Provide** a list of words. They may be spelling words, words from the end of a chapter, or just a list you or the students have generated.

2. **Examine** words in order to find reasons for grouping them together.

3. **Write** down words that seem to fit in a group of their own.

4. **Label** each group of words.

5. **Look** at the words again and try to group them in different ways.

6. **Explore** how the groups can be combined to form larger groups.

Listed below are words used by meteorologists. Imagine you have been invited to spend a weekend with meteorologists and your challenge is to group and label the following words. You could win a trip to the Virgin Islands! You have five minutes.

Absolute Zero	Equinox
Altitude	Faulting
Anticline	Ozone
Anticyclone	Permafrost
Bar	Taiga
Continental Drift	Talus
Cordillera	Temperature Inversion
Cyclone	Turbulence
Dew Point	

Unlocking New Words
The Sound, Structure, Content, Dictionary (SSCD) Approach

Textbook passages often include many words that are not in students' vocabularies. Some words will be new to some students even when the material has been carefully selected for a given grade level. One way to help students with unfamiliar words is to teach the SSCD approach. The SSCD approach to unfamiliar words is not intended as a single lesson. Practice in the method should be provided through prereading activities or in advance organizers that precede the chapters to be covered. With consistent practice, students may learn to use this approach when doing independent studying. The approach consists of the following:

Sound—Some "new" words may not be recognized in print, but they may be familiar when heard. Try to sound them out.

Structure—Look at the separate parts of the new word. Prefixes, suffixes, and roots may be familiar and can help unlock the meaning.

Context—Guess at meaning using clues in the surrounding passage.

Dictionary—If you're still not sure, the word can be found in the text's glossary (where applicable) or dictionary.

Context Clues

One word can have a variety of meanings, which often makes it difficult for students to understand what they are reading. Research has shown that the 500 words most used in the English language have 14,070 separate meanings—an average of 28 meanings per word (*Clearing House*, May, 1982). A student exercise is presented on page 72 to enable students to identify multiple meanings found in vocabulary words by the context clues around them. As an example, look at the following definitions for the single word **break**:

break into pieces	smash
break eggs	separate
break a leg	fracture
break a leg	wishing luck
break a toaster	render inoperable
breakout	escape
breakout	become covered with
break a strike	end by force
break the law	violate
break train of thought	disrupt
break a horse	train to obey
break rank	destroy order of
break a set of books	destroy completeness of
break your fall	lessen force of
break your spirit	weaken or destroy
break your heart	overwhelm
break someone	cause to lose money
break a dollar	give equivalent change for
break a record	surpass
break a story	make known
breakthrough	find a solution
break a circuit	open

break into pieces	come apart
break a fever	diminish
break the surface	emerge above
break into song	begin abruptly
breakup	end
break up	laugh
break up	cry
break bread	eat
break camp	pack up
break in	enter forcibly
break in on	interrupt
break off	discontinue
break of day	opening or beginning
coffee break	interruption or interval
break in the weather	sudden change
all the breaks	chance occurrences
break (in pool)	opening shot
break the bank	win all the money
tax break	advantage
breakdown	emotional state
breakdance	street dance

As you can see, vocabulary words can be extremely confusing.

Student Exercise

Ten sentences are provided on this page, each containing the word **block**. Decide on a definition (you may need a dictionary) for each sentence based on how the word block is used. Write your definition under each sentence.

1. I walk six blocks to school every day.

    block:_____

2. The painting sold for $1,000 on the auction block.

    block: _____

3. We have a butcher block table in the kitchen.

    block: _____

4. Jeremy used suntan lotion to block out ultraviolet rays.

    block: _____

5. Kathy has a mental block against listening.

    block: _____

6. The tackle threw an illegal block.

    block: _____

7. The baby sat quietly on the floor and played with her blocks.

    block: _____

8. The prisoner was assigned to cell block 'C.'

    block: _____

9. Paul loaded the hay into the barn using a block and tackle.

    block: _____

10. "Be quiet or I'll knock your block off!"

    block: _____

Roots and Affixes

Many words are created by grouping word parts together. If students know the meanings of parts of the word, they may be able to deduce what the word means. Ten Latin and two Greek roots lie at the heart of over 2,000 English words (see Figure 16).

FIGURE 16

	Roots		English Example
Latin	facio	(do, make)	**fac**ile, **fac**ility
	duco	(lead, bring forth)	con**duct**
	tendo	(stretch)	ex**tend**
	plico	(fold)	ex**plic**ate
	mitto	(send)	e**mit**
	pono	(place)	im**pone**
	teneo	(hold, have)	**ten**able
	fero	(carry)	de**fer**, **fer**ry
	capio	(take, seize)	**cap**rice, **cap**itulate
	specio	(see, observe)	**spec**ulate, **spec**tacle
Greek	logos	(speech or thinking)	**log**ical
	grapho	(write)	tele**graph**

Have students find English words with these roots in textbooks, newspapers, and magazines. Review these examples in class. Have students make up sentences using these words—drill and test.

Memory and Review

The sensory storage system operates without conscious effort. If something is noticed because it is momentarily of interest (such as a phone number), it goes into short-term memory and is forgotten once the call is made. If the number is to be retained, it must be rehearsed or associated with prior knowledge before it can be stored in long-term memory. The input will be retained only if rehearsal takes place. The goal of school-related activities is long-term memory. Information cannot be retrieved easily unless it is organized so that associations can be made. This is why study skills and mnemonic skills (memory aids) focus on helping students associate new information with old knowledge, and on providing opportunities to rehearse or practice the associations.

When it comes time to review material students have read or obtained from class lectures, many students just read through their text or notes again and call that reviewing. This is, for most students, passive reviewing. The student will have a better chance of remembering the material if he/she becomes actively involved. In previous sections, we have talked about some ways to get students involved in their learning such as asking questions before they read, paraphrasing information, using a system of highlighting, and making up test questions. This section will contain some other ideas for helping students understand and remember information.

An Effective Way to Teach Vocabulary

Keyword Mnemonic Method

The authors' experiences have shown the keyword mnemonic method to be very effective in teaching vocabulary words. When middle and high school students used the keyword mnemonic method to study 14 difficult vocabulary words for eight minutes, they remembered 82% of the definitions; after two weeks, the retention rate was still 80%. Students not using the method recalled only 21% of the meanings!

The keyword mnemonic method has proven to be an excellent tool for students who have difficulty learning new vocabulary words. It is based on the principle of replacing a difficult association (i.e., between a new vocabulary word and its definition) with two easier associations. This is made possible by the use of a "keyword"—a common word that sounds like part or all of the vocabulary word. For example:

Vocabulary Word	Keyword	Definition
Barrister	**Bear**	**Lawyer**
acoustic link (sound-alike)	imagery link (picture)	

The first association is a sound-alike, acoustic link between the vocabulary word and the keyword. The link is based on the sound the words have in common. The second link is an imagery link. The student makes a mental picture with the keyword and the definition interacting.

In this example, the student might picture a bear in a suit acting like a lawyer. Later, when the student hears or sees the vocabulary word, he/she will remember the keyword that sounds like the vocabulary word (Barrister-Bear). When the student remembers the picture with the keyword (Bear-Lawyer), he/she will then link together the word pairs and recall the definition of the vocabulary word (Barrister-Lawyer).

Bearister

Utilizing the Keyword Method

1. Select a list of vocabulary words and their definitions (preferably synonyms). Words with concrete, visualizable meaning work best. A good list length is 15 words.

2. Choose a keyword for each vocabulary word. A keyword should sound as much like the vocabulary word as possible. Ideally it will sound like the first syllable. It should be easy to form a memorable image connecting the keyword and the definition. Concrete words that can be pictured work best.

3. Teach your students the keyword method. You might call the keyword a "linking word" (like a link in a chain). Use several examples. Tell them the keywords to use and the images to visualize.

4. Have your students use the keyword method to study the vocabulary list. Tell and show them a vocabulary word, its keyword, and the definition. Be sure they clearly see a mental picture before you move on to the next word.

5. When testing the list, present each vocabulary word and ask the students to recall both the keyword and the definition.

Keyword Method Vocabulary List

The following is an example to demonstrate how to develop keywords (acoustic links) and their imagery links:

Vocabulary Word	Keyword	Image	Definition
Electorate	Electricity	Voters lined up at the voting booth getting an electric shock.	Voters
Edifice	Face	A building crashing on its own face.	Building
Duct	Duck	A duck stuck in a concrete pipe.	Pipe
Apex	Ape	An ape sitting on two boards that make a point.	Point
Lexicon	Mexican	A Mexican with a dictionary in his backpack.	Dictionary
Citadel	City Bell	An army attacks a fortress when the city bell rings.	Fortress
Palisade	Palace	A palace with a big, tall fence around it.	Fence
Fife	Five	A flute with little fives coming out of it.	Flute
Ague	Egg	An egg with a thermometer in its mouth complaining how hot it is.	Fever

Mnemonic Instruction—Remembering Facts

Research has shown mnemonic instruction to be effective in teaching students to remember content-area facts. The following example of learning with mnemonics is from a unit on minerals. The object of the lesson is for students to remember the color, use, and hardness of different minerals. The students should first be taught concrete rhyming peg words for the numbers one through ten:

one	=	bun	six	=	sticks
two	=	shoe	seven	=	heaven
three	=	tree	eight	=	skate
four	=	door	nine	=	sign
five	=	hive	ten	=	hen

For the mineral **apatite**, the students could be shown this picture and the corresponding data.

Apatite (ape):

- Hardness level five
- Brown color
- Used for fertilizer

The students are then taken through the following steps:

1. The sound association, or keyword for **apatite** is **ape**. The students are directed to remember the picture of a big brown ape pouring a bag of fertilizer on a beehive.

2. The retrieval process should be rehearsed by asking questions such as:

   - "What number is **apatite** on the hardness scale?"
   - "First think of the word clue for **apatite—ape**. Now go back to the picture with the **ape** in it . . . ."
   - "What's happening in the picture?"
   - "Find the peg word, hive—what's the number associated with it?"
   - "What is happening in the picture that reminds you about the use of **apatite**?"

Associations

A great deal of research has found that images are the single most important factor determining free recall. William James found that the mind of man is an "association machine." This means that if we want to learn anything new we should associate it with something we already know. Another educator, Samuel Johnson, found that the main art of memory is the "art of attention." We tend to remember the unusual and forget the common and mundane. Thus, relating facts, information, vocabulary words, etc., to something ridiculous and unusual will enable students to remember and understand.

Word Clues

Single word clues are also helpful in remembering things. For example:

The Great Lakes:	Directions:
H uron	**N** orth
O ntario	**E** ast
M ichigan	**W** est
E erie	**S** outh
S uperior	

Silly Sentences

To remember rules for math, grammar, etc., encourage students to make up silly sentences that can be easily memorized and visualized. The following are eleven examples that illustrate how silly sentences can aid in memorization:

1. Silly sentences can be used to remember the conversion rules for changing big units into equivalent smaller units.

    Hours to Minutes (60 minutes x 3 hours =)
    Pounds to Ounces (16 ounces x 4 pounds =)
    Meters to Centimeters (100 cm x 5 meters =)

    In order for students to remember the conversion rule—**B**ig to **S**mall . . . **M**ultiply—have them picture and remember the phrase, "***Big Students March***"

2. To remember small things renamed as equivalent larger units—**S**mall to **B**ig . . . **D**ivide—have students picture and memorize, "***Saint Bernards Drive.***"

This mnemonic device also works for remembering information in other content areas. Most children learned the names of the lines of the treble clef in music by remembering "***Every Good Boy Does Fine***." It can work just as well for organizing and remembering other information.

3. If students need to remember the first six governors of Oklahoma—*Hard Candy Will Rot Wooden Teeth*.

    Charles **H**askell
    Lee **C**ruce
    Robert **W**illiams
    James Brooks **R**obertson
    John **W**alton
    Martin **T**rapp

4. To spell "geography"—*George Elliott's Oldest Girl Rode A Pig Home Yesterday*.

5. To remember the first five Presidents of the United States in order—*Whales Always Juggle Mice & Monkeys*.

    Washington
    Adams
    Jefferson
    Madison
    Monroe

6. The seven continents—*Elvis Always Ate Apples Alone, Never Sharing*.

    Europe
    Australia
    Africa
    Antarctica
    Asia
    North America
    South America

7. To recall planets in order from the sun—*My Very Educated Mother Just Served Us Nine Pizzas*.

    Mercury
    Mars
    Uranus
    Venus
    Jupiter
    Neptune
    Earth
    Saturn
    Pluto

The following are additional examples of various mnemonic devices for different subject areas:

8. Chemistry

Element	Symbol	Memory Cue
Lead	PB	Plumbers Use Lead Pipes
Tin	SN	Tin Snips
Silver	AG	Silver Hair with Old Age
Potassium	K	A Kettle is a Pot

9. To memorize the seven principles of capitalism—*Fuzzy People Feel So Good Petting Caterpillars.*

   Freedom of Enterprise
   Private Property
   Freedom of Contract
   Savings Leads to Investment
   Government's Role as Umpire
   Profit Motive
   Competition

10. To recall historical events and dates—

   Lincoln-Douglas Debates, 1858
   Lincoln Inaugurated President, 1861
   Lincoln Assassinated, 1865

   Poem Cue:

   Lincoln Debate in Fifty-Eight
   Lincoln's the one in Sixty-One
   Lincoln alive in Sixty-Five?

11. To remember the states, use these silly sentences:

   • *Washington Only Came North In Mountain Wilderness Until Carl Ate Noodle Macaroni* (corresponds to number 1 in Figure 17).

   Washington
   Oregon
   California
   Nevada
   Idaho
   Montana
   Wyoming

Utah
Colorado
Arizona
New Mexico

- *Tilly Only Kept Nuts, Sour Dates, New Donuts* (corresponds to number 2 in Figure 17).

Texas
Oklahoma
Kansas
Nebraska
South Dakota
North Dakota

Here are the sentences for the rest of the sections of states. See if your students can name them all and match them to the map pictured in Figure 17:

- *Minnie Invented Many Articles Lovingly* (corresponds to number 3 in Figure 17).

- *Wise Mich Invited Indians Only Keeping Ten Missing Allies* (corresponds to number 4 in Figure 17).

- *Maine Never Heard Very Many Catchy Radical Ideas* (corresponds to number 5 in Figure 17).

- *Penny's New Years New Jersey Was Very Much Desired* (corresponds to number 6 in Figure 17).

- *Virginia Now Can Sew Corn, Grain, Flowers* (corresponds to number 7 in Figure 17).

FIGURE 17

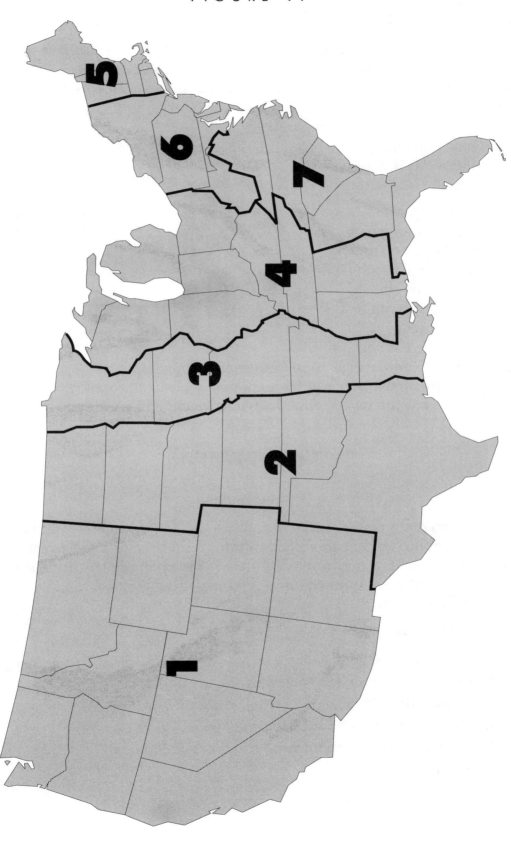

Learning Logs

Learning Logs or Content Journals are an excellent way for students to review and evaluate the material read or covered in class. Typically, students make entries into their logs two or three times a week. By writing down ideas and concepts they've learned, as well as questions about concepts they don't understand, students are better prepared to integrate new concepts with what they already know. This in turn enables students to retain information for future use.

If Learning Logs are going to be effective, they need to be reciprocol undertakings. As the teacher, you need to respond to what is written, think of this response as dialogue, yet try to avoid comments like "Good job" or "Keep trying." Here is an excellent example for Learning Log instructions prepared by a chemistry and anthropology teacher. "Think" Writing explains what she wants, why she wants it, and when it should be done.

"Think" Writing

Chemistry Log

The writing you'll do in your Chemistry Log will provide a way for you to think about what you're learning, to question what you don't understand, and to integrate new concepts and ideas with what you already know. This writing will be **thinking** on paper; therefore, don't worry about mechanical correctness or spelling. Deal with ideas and questions instead.

"Think" writing means:

- Summarizing what you've learned.
- Integrating new ideas with ones you already understand.
- Questioning the significance of what you learn.
- Discovering questions about what you know.
- Discovering questions about what you don't understand.

"Think" writing will help you:

- Understand new material.

- Ask relevant questions.
- Make new knowledge part of you.
- Retain what you learn.
- Improve your ability to write in all subjects.

When should you write? Write when:

- You're confused. Write to discover what specific points you don't understand.
- New concepts are introduced.
- You question the importance of an idea.
- You're preparing for a test.
- You're relaxed and in the mood to write.

The students will need to be assured this is only "thinking" on paper, so they don't need to be too concerned about correctness or spelling. It should be ungraded, except to note that something was written. Students may need to be guided into using Learning Logs by discussing, as a group, concepts, ideas, and questions that might be written in the logs. The following are some suggestions of questions that students can ask themselves:

- What did I learn today?
- What words in science caught my attention?
- (Reaction to class activities.) What did I think of the film, test, etc.? Was it valuable?
- How can I explain the assignment in my own words.
- How did today's information on minerals fit in with what I already know?

Here are some sample entries and responses:

- **Student's Entry:** We studied about **passive** voice today. Passive voice reminds me of lying in a hammock on a summer day with no energy and not a care in the world. You just lie there and let the wind rock you. You just take life as it comes. You have to be indifferent because you don't have any control at all.

  Teacher's Comment: Well, Jamie, what happens if you get thirsty lying in the hammock? Can you do anything about it and retain passive voice?

- **Student's Entry:** I liked our lesson about **organs** today. I was surprised that a leaf is an organ. I knew that lungs and hearts and things like that are organs. But I sure didn't know that hands and arms and tree roots were organs. And why isn't the liver a gland if it can make things our body needs? Our book said a gland is a tissue that can produce different substances.

Teacher's Comment: One difference, Carol, is that glands are tissues while organs are groups of tissues. But we'll go over the differences again. Keep telling me when you're confused.

Study Guides

Many teachers provide study guides for their students. Some are to be filled in by the student, others summarize the material in an orderly fashion. The following are some guidelines for constructing study guides which will enable students to use the guides for effective study:

1. If possible, study guides should be typed (double-spaced).

2. Space and lines should be provided right after the question.

3. The page number on which the answers can be found should be noted.

4. Vocabulary words and terms should be underlined.

5. Watch readability.

6. Abstract concepts should be made as clear as possible.

7. Drawings may help visual and kinesthetic learners (although auditory learners may find them difficult).

8. Present in smaller groups, rather than the entire class.

Sample study guides are included in Figures 18-21. They are the following:

- A **traditional study guide** (Figure 18) for Oklahoma History that has been organized sequentially with the textbook page numbers provided.

- A **textbook study guide** (Figure 19) that has been adapted. The readability has been reduced and each completion item is on a separate line, making the question clearer.

- A **self-monitoring study guide** (Figure 20) that summarizes the chapters and provides an opportunity for students to quiz themselves. This self-checking format lets students know where they need to spend more time.

- A **cloze study guide** (Figure 21) using a chapter summary.

The cloze procedure was developed by Wilson Taylor in 1953 and is based on the psychological theory of closure. This theory states that a person instinctively wants to complete any pattern which is not completed. Use of the cloze procedure will help students develop the ability to handle the fill-in-the-blank variety of tests. It motivates students to read a passage more carefully. Practice in using the cloze procedure is especially effective with chapter summaries. It is an excellent technique for improving students' reading skills as well as content-area knowledge. Students learn to use context (meaning) clues to identify words.

The cloze procedure is simple to use. You simply copy the passage and omit every seventh word. For simple passages, every fifth word might be omitted, and for more difficult passages, every ninth word might be omitted. The first and last sentences are left intact. The students then attempt to fill in as many of the blanks as they can. Any good synonym is acceptable.

Other uses of the cloze procedure:

- Vocabulary terms are omitted.
- Particular parts of speech are omitted (i.e., delete all verbs, or nouns, etc.).
- Prefixes and suffixes are omitted.
- Historical dates are omitted.
- Mathematical concepts and terminology are omitted.
- Proper names and places are omitted.

Students can use the cloze passages when working independently, or as a group while you read the body of the passage and students fill in the blanks. If the terms are essential, the students can silently read the body of the passage as you read aloud the correct term while using the chalkboard or an overhead.

FIGURE 18
Sample Traditional Study Guide

Chapter 17
Oklahoma History

Page 230

1. When was the name Oklahoma officially used?

    _____

2. What does the name Oklahoma mean?

    _____

Pages 230 and 233

3. What were the provisions of the Enabling Act?

    _____

    _____

    _____

    _____

    _____

    _____

    Note: The Enabling Act required that certain definite provisions (or conditions) be included in the state Constitution.

Pages 236-239

4. What were the provisions to be included in the state Constitution?

    _____

    _____

    _____

    _____

    _____

FIGURE 19
Sample Textbook Study Guide

Matter of the Lithosphere, Chapter 4
Completing Ideas

Fill in the blanks using these words:

amorphous	luster	rock-formers
composition	metamorphic	sedimentary
crystal	mineraloid	silicon
igneous	organic	solid
lithosphere	oxygen	weathering

1. The earth's crust is the _____ .

2. The most common element is _____ .

3. The next most common element is _____ .

4. If you can see the atomic pattern, the mineral is a _____ .

5. _____ minerals do not have a crystal form.

6. They should be called _____ , not minerals.

7. Minerals are always _____ .

8. Minerals are not _____ .

9   If minerals reflect light, they have metallic _____ .

10. Each mineral always has the same _____ .

11. Twelve of the common minerals are called _____ .

12. All rocks come from _____ rock.

13. _____ changes rocks at the surface of the earth.

14. Rocks that harden near the surface are called _____ .

15. Rocks that are changed by great heat and pressure are called

_____ .

FIGURE 20
Sample Self-Monitoring Study Guide

Understanding the World, Chapter 18
Eastern Europe and Asia

1.	Rulers of Russia.	1.	Czars
2.	Rulers who run the government as they wish.	2.	Absolute Monarchs
3.	Many _____ became serfs.	3.	Peasants
4.	Changing a country so that it is more like Western Europe.	4.	Westernization
5.	A czar who wanted Westernization.	5.	Peter the Great
6.	A czar who gave nobles more power.	6.	Catherine the Great
7.	This czar freed the serfs.	7.	Alexander II

1.	The Southeastern part of Europe.	1.	Balkans
2.	The _____ Empire ruled the Balkans.	2.	Ottoman
3.	Love and loyalty for a country.	3.	Nationalism
4.	These people won their freedom from the Ottoman Empire.	4.	Greeks
5.	The _____ War started between the Russians and the Ottomans.	5.	Crimean

1.	Having little or nothing to do with other countries.	1.	Isolationism
2.	Secret trading that is against the law.	2.	Smuggling

1.	A dangerous drug made from poppies.	1.	Opium
2.	The British beat the Chinese in the _____ War.	2.	Opium
3.	When one country controls trade in a part of another country.	3.	Sphere of influence
4.	A plan that said that all countries could have the right to trade with China.	4.	Open Door Policy
5.	An uprising by the Chinese against foreign people.	5.	Boxer Rebellion

FIGURE 21

Example Master Copy (place in left side of file folder)

The Monroe Doctrine

In 1823, President Monroe stated a doctrine that has become a key part of our foreign policy. He said that the Americas were no longer open for the setting up of new European colonies. Thus, our country had won an important place in the world. In these years, the number of our people grew to 23,000,000.

Our frontier moved to the West. Each grew in its own way. In the South, plantation life became most important. In New England and the Middle States, people turned to manufacturing and trade.

More and more people moved west to find new farm lands. These people were hardy. They suffered on the trail as they went west; they fought Indians; they tamed the wilderness. In time, they made new lives for themselves. Thus, better transportation made it easier for East and West to trade and travel.

Example Cloze Copy (place in right side of file folder)

The Monroe Doctrine

In 1823, President _____ stated a doctrine that has become a key part of our _____ policy. He said that the Americas were no longer open for the setting up of new _____ colonies. Thus, our country had won an important place in the world. In these years, the number of our people grew to _____.

Our frontier moved to the _____. Each grew in its own way. In the _____, plantation life became most important. In _____ _____ and the _____ _____, people turned to manufacturing and trade.

More and more people moved west to find new _____ lands. These people were hardy. They suffered on the trail as they went _____; they fought _____; they tamed the _____. In time, they made new lives for themselves. Thus, better transportation made it easier for East and West to trade and travel.

Cover and Write Study Technique

One method for individual, active review is the cover and write study technique. Rather than writing the word, date, name, or information over and over to review (as many students do), the student is able to:

- **Check** his/her own learning.
- **Eliminate** learned material.
- **Flag** information needing additional work.

Students may find the cover and write study technique helpful when studying spelling or any other rote material. The steps for students to study with this technique are as follows:

1. Look at the word.

2. Cover it up.

3. See if you can write the word without looking.

4. Look at the word.

5. Check to see if you got the word right.

6. If you did, go on to the next word.

7. If you didn't, look at the word again and either sound it out by syllables or visualize it.

8. Then cover the word again.

9. See if you can write the word without looking now.

10. Look at the word to check if you got the word right.

11. If you still got it wrong, circle or check the word and go on to the next word or task.

12. When you are finished with the list, go back and practice writing the word(s) you missed.

See-Thru Study Sheets

See-thru study sheets may be used to review concepts that the students have been exposed to previously. This technique provides immediate feedback, takes a minimum of time to implement, and can be easily completed by students. It is also extremely inexpensive. The technique is based on the fact that red college theme binders (acetate type) effectively screen out pink and yellow water-based highlighter pens. Thus see-thru study sheets are extremely effective for review or re-teaching of content-area material and make excellent independent study guides. Students can easily use see-thru study sheets to quiz themselves on any type of information, providing immediate feedback.

To make see-thru study sheets, write problems or questions on either standard size paper or on index cards using a dark marker. Write the answers with either a pink or yellow water-based marker. When the study sheet paper or cards are under the plastic theme cover, only the problems or questions are visible. The answers appear when the paper or cards are pulled out from under the theme cover. (We recommend that you do not experiment with different colors. These are the only ones we have found that will work!)

Taking Tests

Very few of us, including our students, enjoy taking tests. Anxiety increases and attendance decreases as test day approaches. How many of our students are truly prepared for any given exam?

The following pages contain many hints for taking tests. These pages are written directly to the student and can be distributed to students as a handout packet. Discuss the suggestions and explain to your students the kinds of questions you include on your tests (e.g., mostly essay, multiple choice, matching, fill-in-the-blank). Not only will the students feel that you are being fair with them, they will also know **how** to study for your specific questions.

Tips for Taking Exams

When you take an examination, do the easy questions first.

This is a good technique whether you are writing an essay test or answering questions. Research has shown that tackling easy items first on a test tends to produce better results than doing the difficult items first on the same test. So skim over the test and find where to begin. On an objective test, don't spend a lot of time worrying about a tough item. Skip it and come back to it later. On an essay test, write the easy items first but leave plenty of space so that your answers will be in the correct sequence.

On an essay test, write down something for every item.

Be sure to read the directions. You may be asked to write only part of the items. Then, for each item you select, write something. Don't leave any item blank. The worst that can happen is that you get a zero for the question anyway. But if you write down something—maybe even a little wild and apparently unrelated—you may pick up a few points.

On an essay test, be neat.

Some informal research indicates that to many teachers a neatly written paper is worth about one letter grade more than the exact same paper written in a sloppy, messy sort of way. Look at it this way: You are an instructor and you have read through 30 or 35 essay exams. You are just naturally going to be a little more sympathetic to the student who makes your job easier by writing neatly and clearly. So for an essay test, do the best you can to make the teacher's reading more pleasant. The teacher will probably repay you for your effort.

On objective tests, if you change your mind, change your answer!

Many students think that their first answer to a test item is somehow magically the best. On the basis of that unfounded belief, they rarely change their answers. Perhaps you, yourself, have changed your response to an objective item and found out later that you were wrong. That was such an uncomfortable event that you couldn't forget it. "Never again," you tell yourself, "I'll stick to my first choice." But you probably also changed answers many times and got them right. However, doing that was such a reasonable thing that there was no reason to remember it.

As a matter of fact, the question of whether or not to change answers has been carefully researched. All of the studies, over decades, are quite consistent. They indicate that on the average you can expect to pick up more points that you will have lost by changing answers. So if you change your mind, change your answer.

Perhaps you want to test out this suggestion. If so, you need only to keep careful track of your changes. Check with your answer sheet later to find out how many points you gained and how many points you lost by the changes. Then in the future you can be guided by data, not superstition.

Before the Test

- Try to predict and practice writing the answers to questions that you think will be asked. (Chapter titles and subheadings can be a good source for possible questions.) Check your notes: What topics did the teacher emphasize?

- Know the course jargon. Study the spelling of words that you might use in your answers.

During the Test

- Take a good writing utensil to class. (Teachers appreciate dark lead or ink they can see.) Watch your handwriting, spelling, and writing mechanics during the test.

- Read quickly through all the questions before beginning to write. Estimate the time you can allow for each question.

- Plan to answer all the questions that you know first. Begin each answer on a separate page, keeping them in order.

- Read the general test instructions. (You may have options as to how many questions you must answer.)

- Be sure to read each question carefully to determine what is really being asked. Sketch an outline in the margin or on scrap paper making sure that all the important points are included in your answer and that they follow a logical order.

- Avoid answers that begin: "It is when . . . " and "It is because . . . ." (Who knows what "it" is referring to?)

- When writing your essay answers, start a separate paragraph for each of the main ideas or statements within one essay answer. Put your details and examples under their respective main ideas. This aids organization and writing mechanics.

- Read over your paper before you turn it in. Check for completeness in expression and ideas and for mechanical errors.

- Use all of your test time. Leave only when the teacher makes you.

After the Test

To improve your test-taking skills, go over all returned papers carefully. Observe your shortcomings and mistakes so that you will not make the same ones on later tests.

Tips for True-False Tests

Do you panic or feel confused when faced with a true-false test? Would knowing some "tricks of the study skills trade" make you feel more confident? Then learn the strategy below and apply it during your next true-false test.

SCORER is an acronym for a series of steps that can improve your ability in passing and/or raising your grade on true-false tests. SCORER stands for:

- ## S = SCHEDULE Your Time

    At the beginning of the test, estimate quickly how much time you can allow for each question. Stick to this estimate. Don't get hung up on just one difficult item. (To estimate time, divide the available test time by the number of questions, such as 60 minutes ÷ 60 questions = 1 minute per question.)

- ## C = CLUE Words

    Paying attention to clue words in true-false statements can help you choose the correct answer even when you are unsure of the subject matter:

    - Statements are usually false when they contain clue words which indicate that the statement must always be true with no exceptions. (Such words include: all, every, none, always, invariably, never, best, exactly, worst.)

    - Statements are usually true when they contain clue words which modify the absoluteness of the statement. (Such clue words include: many, most, some, few, often, usually, sometimes, seldom, more, equal, less, good, bad.)

    - Watch out for statements that are really definitions, such as: "All triangles have three sides." (This is a true statement: be careful of these statements in science and math areas.)

- ## O = OMIT Difficult Questions Until Last

    Answer the easy questions first as you go through your test and place a mark by the doubtful statements. This action will help you stick to your time schedule; will ensure your receiving points on all the items you know; and may trigger your memory when going back to answer the doubtful statements on the test. Repeat this procedure until all the questions are answered. (**Hint:** On tests that count only the correct answers in the score or for tests that do not penalize for wrong answers, **always** give an answer. The percentages are on your side for picking up some points even through guessing.)

- ## R = READ Each Question Carefully

    Reading each true-false statement carefully (and the test instructions) can sometimes make or break your test score:

    – Remember to interpret true-false statements as they are stated. Don't become emotionally involved with statements so that you are reading more into the statement than there is.

    – Also remember that all parts of true-false statements must be completely true or false.

- **E =ESTIMATE Answers (Use Intelligent Guessing)**

  Most objective tests are scored by counting only your correct answers. (But be sure this is the way your test will be scored before applying the intelligent guessing strategy.) When you must guess, use all the tips you have learned so far about true-false tests, especially about clue words.

- **R = REVIEW Your Work**

  In your estimated schedule of time to spend on each test question, you should have also allowed a few minutes in which to look back over the entire test. Don't ever leave a test before you must. Check each of your answers—you may have made a careless mistake, but don't change your answers unless you have a good reason.

Tips for Multiple-Choice Tests

- Read through the test quickly, answering only questions that you are sure about. (Many times clues to answers can be found in other questions.)

- Read the entire question and all the possible answers. Sometimes the last answer is the best answer even though other answers might work.

- Read all possible answers, marking through the first letter of those you are pretty sure are not correct. Usually a multiple-choice question will have one correct answer, two that are distractors, and one that is definitely wrong.

- Locate the distractors. Sentences with the words "always," "never," "none," and "all" are often distractors—but not every time. Be careful.

- If you can find one or two of the distracting answers to a question, then look closely at them as they may give you the clue to the correct answer. Ask yourself, "What makes this a distractor?" and then select the "best" answer.

- If you have two answer options that you feel are equal, select one and write a brief rationale for your choice in the margin—this is usually good for extra credit, even if the answer is wrong.

- If you change your mind, change your answer on multiple-choice tests.

- On standardized tests, leave unknown questions until last. If you have time, count the number of As, Bs, Cs, and Ds you've already answered. Usually there will be an equal number of each, and odds are that if you have fewer of one letter that will be the one you should tend to select on the remaining questions.

- Never leave a multiple-choice question unanswered. You have at least a 25% chance of getting it correct just by accident. If you can eliminate two choices, you are just as likely to get it right as you are to get it wrong.

- When in doubt, guess B or C. Teachers often try to "hide" the answer.

Tips for Essay Tests

When you take the test:

- Answer the easy questions first.

- Skip the tough questions and come back to them later. Answer the questions that you know first will help you stay calm for the test.

On an essay test:

- **Write Something for Every Question.** Be sure to read the directions. Don't leave the question blank—that means no points for sure.

- **Be Neat.** If you were the teacher, would you want to read 50 or 60 messy papers? Neatness can make a difference in the teacher's grading. It Counts!

Notes:

Things You Can do to Help Your Students Survive

- Write main ideas on chalkboard or use an overhead to alert students to important information.

- Print information on one side of the board at a time . . . walk to the other side and continue. Come back to the first side and erase. Then start over. This gives the students a chance to copy as much information as possible. Make sure what you write is legible.

- If following a text, present information in same order as information in text.

- Provide carbon paper (or NCR paper) and appoint good notetakers to make copies during lectures for students who are having a hard time keeping up.

- Instruct students how you want notes taken in your class.

- One of the least effective ways to teach vocabulary is to have vocabulary lists with definitions. Words are best learned in context and should be presented that way in sentences or thought units.

- Emphasize quantity or quality—not both.

- Record lectures for students to listen to later.

- Outline the work for the entire week, day-by-day, including pages to read, homework assignments, projects, etc. (This helps keep students on track.)

- The ability to read charts and graphs may be skills the students have never acquired. It may be necessary to teach this concept as a separate skill.

- Use operation definitions (e.g., "What is it used for" can be effective). Remember to evaluate on this basis too.

The FORCE Strategy

The FORCE strategy was developed to provide a systematic means for students to approach studying for a test. The strategy is outlined below:

Find Out—When the teacher announces a test, ask questions:

- "What will the test cover?"
- "What types of questions will be asked?"

Organize—Collect all materials you can for taking the test:

- Notes, old tests, books, etc.

Review—Skill chapters, charts, maps, summaries, questions, or vocabulary; highlight notes, review old tests and assignments

Concentrate—Make a study sheet (cue sheet) by putting important information in question/answer form.

Early Exam—Practice by pretesting yourself:

- Take turns asking questions with a partner.
- Take your own test from your study sheet.
- Use the cover and write study technique (see page 92).

The following is a quick reference for students stumped by unknown words:

A **strategy** is a purposeful method of solving a problem. Strategies for unknown words:

Look it up
Ask someone
Use context clues
Structural analysis
Phonetics

Flash! Quizzes, Small-Group Study Aid Learning

A study at Harvard University concludes that frequent quizzes, homework assignments, and small-group study can substantially increase academic achievement. Richard J. Light, the study's author, aimed the study at higher education, but states that the results could also be applied to the secondary school level. The study found that most students appreciated the courses that provided quick and frequent feedback in the form of quizzes, tests, short papers, and homework. This gave students an opportunity to check their learning more often and get criticism and assistance before the final grade was given on an assignment.

The study also found a "clear payoff" in dividing students into small study groups of four to six students. According to the researchers, small-group study creates enthusiasm for classwork and improves student achievement. Through this method, students learn how to keep a group moving toward completion of a task and how to include all members in a discussion.

One-Minute Paper

(This is another great idea from the Harvard University study conducted by Mr. Light.)

The Harvard study recommended feedback for instructors in the form of a daily "one-minute paper." The idea is to leave the last minute or two of class to allow students to take out a sheet of paper and jot down what they consider to be the main point of the day's lesson. Students should also be encouraged to write down any unanswered questions they still have. The "one-minute paper" encourages students to think throughout the class about what they will write. This method also provides the teacher with some valuable feedback about how they are getting their main ideas across to the students. Some instructors involved in the study began their lectures with a brief discussion of the one-minute papers submitted in the previous session. This allowed the students to see what the entire group found clear and unclear, and whether their own questions were shared by others.

Spelling

The time to teach spelling is during the editing stage of the writing process. Most of us make careless mistakes when writing rough drafts but correct them during the editing phase. However, students experiencing difficulty with writing and spelling do not realize their errors. Too often, the editing stage of the writing process falls on the shoulders of the teacher. Teachers circle spelling and other errors, or meticulously print "sp" above each error. As a result, the teacher becomes adept at spotting spelling errors, while the students remain at the same skill level as before the papers were written. Here are some suggested tactics to involve students in editing their own work:

- When errors occur, you must first determine whether the students have made genuine errors, or if the misspellings are the results of carelessness. One way to determine this is to put a check mark at the beginning of the lines in which the errors occur. The students should then try to find the misspelled words. If they do not find the error, it is then placed on their individual lists of words to learn.

- Implement peer editing. Students who are asked to be aware of others' spelling will ultimately become more critical of their own work.

- The most effective way for students to learn to spell is to correct their own tests.

- If students miss too many, divide the lists in half, have them learn five, then ten, etc.

- Give students a "spelling conscience"—that correct spelling is a necessary skill that will help them throughout their lives.

- Tell them how to spell a word when they ask. Don't tell them to sound it out or spell it the best they can. (If they could have done that, they wouldn't have asked you!)

- Set up a "word bank" for their own reference in a spiral notebook or on file cards.

- Teach students to use a dictionary by making an educated guess.

Student Strategies for Independent Spelling

The following strategies will enable students to improve their spelling in a self-directed fashion:

Guess and Test

- **Guess** the spelling of the word and write it down.
- **Test** your spelling by looking it up in the dictionary.

Simplify the Problem

- Say the word.
- Listen for a word or sound in the word that you already know how to spell.
- Write part of the word that you know how to spell.
- Guess and test the rest of the word.

Make a List

- Say the word.
- Make a list of all the possible ways you could spell the word.
- Look at your list and decide which word looks correct.

- Take the word that looks correct to you and look it up in the dictionary.
- If you can't find it, try a second choice.

Listen for Sounds

- Say the word.
- Listen for all the sounds you hear in the word.
- Write those sounds down in the order that you hear them.
- Look up the word you've made in the dictionary.
- If you can't find it, try a second choice.

Find a Pattern

- Say the word.
- Do you know a word that rhymes with the word you are trying to spell?
- Use this rhyming word to help you spell and remember the original vocabulary word.

Adapting Assignments

Students are often assigned the task of writing reports. Students with difficulties in reading or written expression may turn in partial or incomplete reports, or may not even make an attempt to do an assignment. Report writing is not an easy task for these students, even when they know the material. In addition, other students may experience anxiety when assigned an oral report. If all students are given several options instead of a standard format for reports, they may show greater interest, motivation may be higher, and you will probably find that the quality of your students' reports has improved. The following is a list of 32 different alternative ways to complete a report:

1. **Selling a Book, Idea or, Concept**—Students try to convince the rest of the class that their idea is the best.

2. **Radio Broadcast**—Students act as newscasters reporting exciting events into a tape recorder.

3. **Panels**—Panels can be formed by several students reporting on the same topic.

4. **Character Letter Exchange**—Letters are exchanged between students playing different characters from textbooks, novels, or plays. The letters are written in character.

5. **Letters**—The students write letters to authors, athletes, politicians, and local community and civic leaders.

6. **Different Endings**—The students respond to the question: Could the event or story have ended differently? How?

7. **Code**—Reports can be written in code with a key included.

8. **New Stories**—Reports can be written in newspaper format with headlines and student bylines.

9. **Illustrate**—Students draw, paint, etc. a sequence of events or experiments.

10. **Critiques**—Students write reviews on topics, events, or experiments.

11. **Make Models of Things**—Some examples include: The White House, wireless radio, molecules.

12. **Make a Display**—Students build displays that correlate with an era, culture, event, or experiment.

13. **Paint a Mural**—Students depict sequences of events. Example: The "Trail of Tears" or the birth of a chicken.

14. **Make a Large Map**—Students create a map illustrating the action of a story, where the events took place, etc. The map is used as a visual as students orally describe the story.

15. **Make a Poster**—To advertise or sell a book, event, or concept to the class.

16. **Create a Crossword Puzzle**—Students give a short oral report and have the class solve the puzzle.

17. **Make a Collage**—A collage made from various materials to illustrate a concept or key idea from a lesson.

18. **Make a Filmstrip**—Students make a film or video and use a projector or VCR to show it.

19. **Diaries**—Students write diaries as if they were characters from a lesson text.

20. **Dramatize**—Students act out an interesting or exciting incident from a text.

21. **Make a Bulletin Board Display**—Students create a display for the classroom or school hall.

22. **Develop a Visual Timeline**—Students make a timeline to illustrate a biographical sketch or historical event.

23. **Demonstrate**—Students perform experiments and document each phase.

24. **Travel Talk**—Students give talks about a state or county trip they have taken using words, pictures, and maps.

25. **Make a Mobile**—Students visually depict a story by using pictures or renderings of characters from texts.

26. **Dress Up**—Students imitate personas of different characters from class texts, while the audience tries to guess who they are depicting.

27. **Riddles**—Students write riddles about concepts or ideas and give hints where to find the answers.

28. **Pro/Con Panel**—Organize a pro and con panel that consists of some students who liked a concept or lesson and some who did not.

29. **Individual Conferences**—You have individual conferences with students to talk about themes and concepts learned.

30. **Telegrams**—Students compose telegrams, trying to give the "message" in 15 words or less.

31. **Poetry**—Students write original poems about an event, character, problem, or idea.

32. **Reading**—Students read aloud their favorite sections from class texts.

Appendix

Readability (Fry Formula)

The Fry Formula is recommended because of its simplicity and accuracy, **especially for secondary level materials**. Most publishers of low-readability versions of textbooks use the Spache or Dale-Chall Formula. These formulas usually yield a lower estimate when used on secondary texts. This is due to the fact that they eliminate proper nouns in calculating readability. They also assume that the students have a working sight vocabulary. Elimination of proper nouns is inappropriate for secondary texts, since the students are required to learn those terms.

Students are often assigned reading material in magazines. It is wise to check the readability of any material that is assigned. Some readability levels for popular magazines are as follows (levels may vary with different issues of the periodical):

- *Time*—College Level
- *U.S. News and World Report*—College Level
- *Reader's Digest*—12th Grade
- *Saturday Evening Post*—11th Grade
- *Cycle*—9th Grade
- *Popular Science*—9th Grade
- *Glamour*—8th Grade

Readability cannot be guessed, it must be calculated. Reading studies reveal that teachers consistently underestimate the reading level of written material.

Most textbooks are written at a reading level that is higher than the grade level indicated on the text. For example, many ninth grade science texts are written at a college reading level. Teachers do not have to rely on the publisher's estimate of the reading level. Anyone can find the reading level of a class text in about 15 minutes by using the following seven steps:

1. Randomly select three passages from the text and count 100 words in each, beginning at the start of a paragraph. One passage should come from the first part of the book, one from the middle, and one from the end. **Do** count proper nouns, initials, acronyms, and numerals. Count contractions and hyphenated words as one word. A word is defined as a group of symbols with a space on either side. Thus, "Joe," "IRA," "1945," and "7,000" are each counted as one word.

2. For each 100-word passage, count the total number of sentences. Estimate the length of the fraction of the last sentence to the nearest tenth.

3. Count the total number of syllables in each 100-word passage. A syllable is defined as a phonetic syllable. Generally, there are as many syllables as vowel sounds. When counting syllables for numerals and initials, count one syllable for each symbol. For example, "1945" is four syllables, "IRA" is three syllables, "$" is one syllable, and "7,000" is four syllables.

4. Find the average number of sentences for the three passages.

5. Find the average number of syllables for the three passages.

6. Plot the average number of sentences and the average number of syllables on Fry's Graph (see page 113). The area where the dot is plotted will give you the approximate grade level.

7. If a great deal of variability is found in the syllable or sentence count, use additional passages to find the averages.

The following reproducible worksheet on page 111 can be used in conjunction with Fry's Graph to summarize the results of the calculations for each of your texts, study guides, or test materials. In addition, the authors have provided a homework plan student handout (see page 115) to use in your classrooms to promote responsibility, accuracy, and overall efficiency among your students. Good luck!

Fry Readability Formula Summaries

Book Title _____ Publisher _____

Grade Level _____ Copyright _____

Subject _____

Passage	page	start	end	syllables	sentences
1.	_____	_____	_____	_____	_____
2.	_____	_____	_____	_____	_____
3.	_____	_____	_____	_____	_____

Total _____   _____

÷3 _____   ÷3 _____

average   average

Readability _____

Book Title _____ Publisher _____

Grade Level _____ Copyright _____

Subject _____

Passage	page	start	end	syllables	sentences
1.	_____	_____	_____	_____	_____
2.	_____	_____	_____	_____	_____
3.	_____	_____	_____	_____	_____

Total _____   _____

÷3 _____   ÷3 _____

average   average

Readability _____

Fry's Graph for Estimating Readability (Extended)
By Edward Fry, Rutgers University Reading Center, New Jersey
Average Number of Syllables per 100 Words

This Homework Plan

Makes me responsible!
Improves accuracy!
Improves grades!
Is faster!

1. What I will study: _____

2. How long I will work: _____

3. How I will review: _____

4. Time I will finish: _____

I am committed to complete my plan!

_____   _____

signature   date

Other Sopris Publications of Interest . . .

Exceptions

—Deborah A. Murphy, Celia C. Meyers,
Sylvia Olesen, Kathy McKean, & Susan H. Custer
Community Services and Dissemination Center, Cushing, Oklahoma

Exceptions is filled with techniques, practical tools, and activities to help classroom teachers meet the needs of mildly disabled middle and high school students. *Exceptions* provides adaptive techniques for modifying regular instructional approaches and materials to accommodate the special needs student.

Included are compensatory instructional techniques and materials in language arts, mathematics, and vocabulary building; remedial techniques and approaches in reading, spelling, and written expression; assessment tools, management forms, lesson plans, tests, and a variety of teaching activities. The activities in *Exceptions* facilitate the mastery of school survival skills (sequential, instructional, and developmental) often underdeveloped in students with learning disabilities.

Better IEPs

—Barbara Bateman, Mary Anne Linden

Better IEPs is a reference every administrator, advocate, school psychologist, special educator, and parent of a child receiving special services should have! This informative book provides educators and parents a powerful tool for writing an IEP that works for the child—one that is both legally correct and educationally useful.

Presented is a powerful three-step IEP process that is child-centered and individualized, rather than program-centered and routinized. The process draws upon Dr. Bateman's decades of experience in special education law. Through her clear interpretation of these laws, parents and educators are provided the confidence and "know-how" to develop IEPs that are worthwhile to educators, understandable to parents, pleasing to compliance monitors, and beneficial to children.

Now in its third edition, *Better IEPs* has been completely updated and revised to include the IDEA Amendments of 1997.

Ideas for Inclusion

—Anne M. Beninghof

Across the country, schools are revising their educational strategies to include students with severe disabilities in the regular classroom setting. In response, teachers with little or no special education background are quickly trying to upgrade their knowledge base and skills in order to experience success with these students.

Ideas for Inclusion: The Classroom Teacher's Guide to Integrating Students With Severe Disabilities provides classroom teachers with 50 practical, easy-to-implement strategies for successfully integrating students with moderate and severe disabilities. The strategies are each just a few pages long, so they can be quickly referenced. Strategy areas include:
- Curriculum and grading modification;
- Classroom management;
- Working with peer tutors, parents, and paraeducators;
- Facilitating friendships; and
- Many more!

In addition, *Ideas for Inclusion* provides a brief overview of the rationale for integration, a review of relevant terminology, and an explanation of important philisophical principles.

Armed with *Ideas for Inclusion*, the classroom teacher will feel more confident and comfortable about including all students in the learning environment. Its easy-to-read format makes it a terrific desk resource for the teacher who wants to quickly find and use a good idea.

Ideas for Inclusion is also helpful to others—special educators, parents, and related professionals—who are promoting and supporting inclusion in schools. Also available is the companion piece geared toward the school administrator, ***Ideas for Inclusion: The School Administrator's Guide***.

Continued

TGIF: But What Will I Do on Monday?

—Susan L. Fister and Karen A. Kemp

TGIF: But What Will I Do on Monday? is a powerful resource for educators, working either alone or collaboratively, to find alternatives for effectively responding to the increasing number of instructional challenges they face in their classrooms. *TGIF* provides solutions for meeting the needs of all students in any classroom setting.

TGIF contains a collection of practical accommodation techniques which respond to needs encountered at four critical points in the instructional process:

- **T**eacher-Directed Instruction
- **G**uided Practice Activities
- **I**ndependent Practice Activities
- **F**inal Measurement

These accommodation techniques are organized in a quick reference format as commonly asked questions, so that educators can simply identify the specific challenge they are facing, locate the most appropriate question under one of the four instructional component headings (either T, G, I, or F), and select one of the many relevant techniques listed. The accommodation techniques are also classified by the level of effort (either low or moderate) necessary for implementation.

TGIF provides a simple guide to making instruction more effective, so that each student is given the opportunity to learn in his or her own way within a caring classroom environment.

Also available is ***TGIF: Making It Work on Monday***, a companion piece containing blackline masters of *TGIF* activities for classroom use.

To order additional copies of *SMARTS,* the other books described,
or for a free catalog, please call toll free

(800)547-6747